To long Time friends David & Jean
Happy Trails
Don Frazier
'99

99·VA-

The Will James Books

The Will James Books

A Descriptive Bibliography for Enthusiasts and Collectors

by
Don Frazier

Foreword
by
A.P. Hays

Dark Horse Associates
Long Valley, NJ
1998

Rocking R
was the Will James brand
and also the name of his
ranch in Montana

Editor: Jacquelyn Sorensen

Book design: J. Wayman Williams Associates
Basking Ridge, NJ
Book was designed on a Macintosh
computer using Pagemaker 6.52.
Text is set in 11 point Bookman light.

CONTENTS

ACKNOWLEDGEMENTS

First, I do certainly thank Will James for being not only a genius but also one of the only writers and artists in the past 100 years who actually wrote and illustrated the ranching West as it truly was. He is also the only one who portrayed pistols as tools rather than as dueling pieces - and very insignificant cowboy tools at that.

There are many who have aided me in this endeavor. My thanks go to the principals of the Will James Art Company of Billings, Montana who have graciously granted permission for the use of the many Will James illustrations shown throughout this book. I am surely in debt to the authors of the three biographies of Will James — Anthony Amaral, William Gardner Bell, and Jim Bramlett. More than thanks go to two of my collaborators on this book and on my previous 'book on books,' *Recognizing Derrydale Press Books*: my bride of 52 wondrous years, Gretchen; and friend, patient advisor, and gifted photographer, Wayman Williams. Also my grateful thanks to my daughter, Jacquelyn Sorensen, professional writer and editor, who spent countless hours advising on and editing the manuscript. Friend Patti Williams gave much time too.

A special thank you goes to my longtime friend, A. P. Hays. Abe knows and loves the books too, but is probably best known as a Western Art critic/expert, and he is positively the most able, knowledgeable, and eloquent lecturer who exists today on the subject of Will James and his art. Over the past 20 years he has taught me many of the details and points that appear in this book, and he has also most kindly agreed to write the Foreword.

FOREWORD

Will James worked in the golden age of American book publishing, competing with artists from the Brandywine School and a virtual renaissance of other outstanding ones during the 1920's and 1930's. The writing field was just as stellar. At his own publisher were the likes of Hemingway, Fitzgerald, and Wolfe. Then, too, there were such earlier giants as Dickens, Grimm, Stevenson, Verne, and Cooper, whose books were reissued as "classics." In this nation's finest of all publishing periods, the work of Will James was praised and his books were successful.

One of the real secrets of his considerable success as an author, of course, was his ability to *both* write and illustrate his own books. In America such a talent, on a broad scale, is unique. A very real means of penetration of one's ideas with the reader is more authoritative when both words and pictures are combined by a single creator. Knowledge and understanding by the reader is enhanced. The veracity of the message is heightened and attitudes are positively affected.

The special feel and flavor in Will James' depictions of the cowboy and his horses originated from his deep comprehension of and respect for the subject matter. His knowledge and insight developed mainly from his participation in cowboy life rather than from an observation of it.

Especially with his early books, Will James was able to permeate his work with an excitement and freshness that both the public and the critics could not miss. He was invariably original in pictures and words and never derivative. He drew in pencil or ink in a technically superb and imaginative fashion which was perfectly united with the content and subject. His gestural (motion or action) abilities in art were of the highest rank and often unsurpassed even today.

In his writing, as the *New York Herald Tribune* critic observed: "He achieved a dignity and simplicity far beyond the reach of nine out of ten professional writers and gave to the world the best reminiscences that have ever come off the ranges..." The graphic nature of his illustrations, when coupled with the truth and sincerity of his own conversational narrative, assured him a devoted following. Many of his readers wrote to him that they were first attracted to his books by the pictures. Scribner's advised him that during the terribly hard Depression years of the 1930's when all book sales were often cut in half, he remained in the top rank of best-selling authors.

Surprisingly, Will James achieved his ranking despite being completely unresponsive in his books to the major emphasis placed by other writers and artists on the more popular and commercial themes of violence. He felt that distorted and marred one's perception of the West and the cowboy. James limited his violence to that between animal and man. And, while man was often a participant, he was generally subordinate to the action. Always, in both words and pictures, James wanted to bring the public perception of cowboys back toward the reality of their workaday existence and away from the false myths so popular in magazines, books, and films. All of James' attitude and talent aimed at providing the public with a truer and more complete comprehension of the cow country. He wanted the life of the cowboy to be appreciated and admired for its realities and values as he understood them. Often the result was, for millions in the United States and other nations, a sense of virtual participation in, rather than merely an observation of, the American West.

Seventy-five years have now passed since Charles Scribner's & Sons published the first short story with drawings by Will James in 1923. After publication of just his first book in 1924, he quickly became established as *the* new authority on cowboy life in both words and pictures. It is a position he continues to hold today among readers old enough to have seen his Scribner's books or later reprint editions by Scribner's, A. L. Burt Company, Grosset & Dunlop, World Publishing Company, Bantam Books, Sun Dial Press, University of Nebraska Press, and most recently, Mountain Press Publishing Company.

For years some of us have privately compiled our own lists of what constitutes a James first edition, and what the keys and abnormalities are. Hardly any of those elite few have tried to keep track of his later reprinted editions. Don Frazier has brought a sincere, formal, and serious approach to the matter. This book will be very useful to the many Will James book collectors and students of his work. For more than ten years Don and I have shared many views about James' books and often with no little specificity. We exchanged ideas and had a mutual respect for the quality of the work. Often we lamented the times we felt Scribner's erred in format or production. Rightfully, Don Frazier comes to this project as a result of his lifetime love of cowboy life and the wild horse. In this he emulates and provides homage to a code and a Western way of life that he and James both value deeply.

A. P. Hays

Arizona West Galleries
Scottsdale
copyright 1998 A.P. Hays

About The Illustrations

My own words about Will James' illustrations start with the firm conviction that he was one of the two best illustrators of the horse in action in the 20th century. The other, who worked primarily in the eastern and European field, was Paul Brown. No one else even comes close to the talent and ability of those two. Will James captures the spirit of the western wild horse and also the bucking bronc as no one else ever has before him or since. A very great many of Will's sketches tell a whole story even without any captions. You can very often tell what the horse is thinking, and the rider too. This is particularly true for anyone who has worked with horses. Pictured here the splayed feet, cocked tail and particularly the head carriage show obdurate

objection to this rider's request for a left turn.

Many of the western artists who have followed him, right on up to today, got much of their inspiration from Will James' work.

Will James could and did draw horses from the pictures in his head. He didn't use photos or any other crutch. He had it all in his mind. He drew with almost perfect anatomical accuracy in every position and motion,

yet he could also add subtle inaccuracies and/or exaggerations to bring out mood and illustrate the written copy that, with the drawings, enlivened his wonderful stories. There are many authenticated stories of his making a full and fine line drawing in just a few minutes. Even starting with ears at one end and a tail at the other and then filling in a properly proportioned and active horse in between!

For the really definitive and very knowledgeable word on Will James' art I do urge you to read 'The Art of Will James' by A. P. Hays. This was first published in *Will James: The Spirit of the Cowboy*, produced in 1985. If it has not been published since, it surely should be. Abe is the recognized expert to authenticate or appraise Will James art works. My book makes comments about the illustrations in Will James' books, but I make no effort to evaluate them from an artistic point of view. Abe Hays does that to perfection and quotes then-contemporary, and more recent, experts and critics who help to bear out Will's genius.

Just a few lines in part from one of Abe's quoted experts, artist Harry Jackson:

"I have loved Remington and Russell all of my life. Their work always inspires me. But one good black and white Will James drawing contains more life-force than all their work, including painting and bronzes, rolled into one. Let me emphasize how much I love and am inspired by everything that Remington and Russell ever did. I'm not knocking them, I'm merely paying the drawing of James its just due... It was his line—his miraculous, energy-packed line and the vibrant drive, thrust, and gesture he captured with that line—that said it all."

AUTHOR'S FIFTH WORD

There have been numerous magazine articles and five good books* written about Will James, the man. This is **not** a sixth one.

This is a book about Will James' **books** and what is in and on them. It is intended for Will James enthusiasts and collectors - and for knowledgeable book dealers as well.

The initial aim and purpose here is to describe the first editions of Will James' 24 titles and 27 books, and to detail the differences where the first edition comes in two or more states. All of Will James' books were first produced by Charles Scribner's Sons. Most were reprinted at least once by Scribner's, and some many times. A number of the titles were reprinted by other publishers through agreements with Scribner's. This book mentions many of the American reprints up to the early 1960s, but makes no claim to have found them all and has made no attempt to trace the foreign language editions, of which there were a considerable number.

An almost entirely self-taught artist and illustrator from an early age, Will James (1892-1942) also was a most imaginative raconteur throughout his cowboying years. "Windy Bill" his admiring campfire cronies frequently called him, but with respect, because he was a 'top hand' in those days.

Will wrote his books much as he had told his 'windy' and true tales in the cow camps: episodes as short stories, strings of episodic stories with a central character running through them, and a few true novels. The novels often had freestanding episodes that were later pulled out and put into books of short stories with only minor changes, if any.

* See last page of this Fifth Word for the five-book list.

His wonderful illustrations could sometimes come close to telling the story all by themselves, so his production with these two talents kept his adoring readers buying everything he turned out until his premature death in 1942, at age 50.

His words and masterful drawings together portray horses, cows, and cowboying to show how life really was on the great ranches of the late 19th and early 20th centuries. There is an occasional picture or story with a gun present, usually something useful like a rifle, but not a single gunfighter or six-gun fight in any of his 24 books. He deplored the 'Shoot-em-Ups' as a total misrepresentation of the cowboy and of ranching as it truly was. Most of the real westerners I knew and worked with felt the same way. *There was more than enough action and danger in the real ranching world to satisfy any plot, and Will James' books show and prove that beyond any doubt.*

The Mountain Press of Missoula, Montana, in conjunction with the Will James Art Co. of Billings, Montana, has embarked on an ambitious schedule of reprinting all of the Will James titles starting with the first book, *Cowboys North and South.* So far at this writing they have produced eight or more and have done a very beautiful job with a lot of them. This is the only mention that I will make about any reprints after about the early 1960s. I have not researched the modern reprint activity, I only know that there has been some of a sporadic nature.

The correct name of Will James' publisher is Charles Scribner's Sons. However at the bottom of the spines of the books and dust jackets they used just the first nine letters — Scribners — without the apostrophe. I refer to the publisher as Scribner's except when describing the name as it appears at the bottom of book and jacket spines.

To keep this work as clear and simple as possible, each book is described with the following format:

Contents: Details whether the volume is a collection of short stories, a novel, or a novelette. When a book of titled short stories, each is listed and briefly described.

Comments: Usually my own biased views, and complimentary, but not always. Scribner's had several instances of very unfortunate editing, as in the *Smoky* Illustrated Classic and the *Will James Book of Cowboy Stories.*

First Edition: Sometimes more than one state. Also it should here be noted that with the first five first-edition Will James books, up through 1929, the first edition did not have the Scribner's 'A' under the copyright. All the subsequent first-edition books, starting with *Lone Cowboy,* 1930 do have the first edition 'A' except one. With *Flint Spears* -1938, the 'A' was inadvertently omitted by Scribner's on its first edition.

Size & Price: Size is in inches and price was the retail price at which the first edition was offered for sale.

Binding: The description of the first edition binding is given. If the binding comes in two or more first-edition states, each one is detailed.

Dust Jacket: Nearly every first edition was issued with a dust jacket and, because it is mentioned so often in this book, I have frequently shortened it to the simple abbreviation: dj.

Pages: The actual numbered pages of the book text, plus the free endpapers.

Illustrations: By quantity, and whether in black and white or in color (black and white is often abbreviated to b&w).

Later Editions: Scribner's reprints are listed first, then other publishers next, Grosset & Dunlap last.

FIVE BIOGRAPHICAL WORKS CONCERNING WILL JAMES
(listed in order of publication date)

1. Amaral, Anthony - *The Gilt Edge Cowboy* (1967) - Los Angeles, Westernlore Press.

2. Amaral, Anthony - *The Last Cowboy Legend* (1980)- Reno, NV, University of Nevada Press.

3. J. M. Neal & A. P. Hays - *Will James: The Spirit of the Cowboy* - (1985)- Casper, WY, Nicolaysen Art Museum.

4. William Gardner Bell - *Will James, The Life and Works of a Lone Cowboy* (1987) - Flagstaff, AZ, Northland Press.

5. Jim Bramlett - *Ride for the High Points* (1987)- Missoula, MT, Mountain Press. (1995) reprinted by Mountain Press.

Some details about the author,
his background and
qualifications (if any),
appear at the back of this
book in the Afterword

The Will James Books

COWBOYS NORTH AND SOUTH
1924

Contents: This, Will James' first book, is a series of short stories about cowboy life in the real and actual West as it truly was between the 1870s and the early years of the 20th century. These stories, in colorful words and striking illustrations, portrayed the true working West rather than the Hollywood variety. All of the eight short stories in the book were previously printed in magazines. Seven of them appeared first in *Scribner's Magazine,* and the last one was first printed in *The Saturday Evening Post.*

Comments: In 1924, when this book appeared, most people young and old knew very little about the actual West and they were hungry to know much more about ranching and about cowboys too. Will James went a long way toward filling this void and his stories and pictures have been treasured by all ages for generations. It is hard to find a first edition of this book in fine condition, and even harder to find one in a fine dust jacket. As Will James' first book, it is an important cornerstone for any serious collector.

First Edition: Cowboys North and South (and all 23 of the titles that followed) was first produced by Charles Scribner's Sons, New York & London. The first edition of this book was produced in two states. Both states have the date, 1924, under the Scribner's name at the bottom of the title page, and that is how to tell that a

1

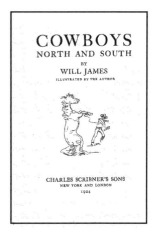

copy is the first edition. All Scribner's later reprints have a later date at the bottom of the title page — or no date.

The second state of the first edition of *Cowboys North and South* is identical to the first state in all details but one: the back of the first half-title page lists two titles: *Cowboys North and South*, <u>and</u> *The Drifting Cowboy*. The title page still says 1924, but *The Drifting Cowboy* wasn't produced until 1925! The obverse of the first half-title page in the first state is blank. Also on the 1925 reprint it is blank. However, on the 1926 reprint edition the two titles are there! I hope you can figure out what was in Scribner's mind. I sure can't.

Size & Price: 9-1/2" high, by 7-1/4" deep, by 1" thick. Price $3.50

Binding: Gray cloth covers and spine with black ink title and author on front cover and spine. It says Scribners at the bottom of the spine. The front cover also has a nice line drawing of a cowboy having just 'front footed' a rearing horse. The line drawing is in red ink and is repeated in black ink on the title page of the book.

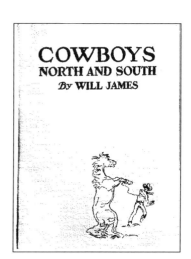

Dust Jacket: Gray paper jacket with a fine black ink drawing of a cowboy on a bucking horse on the front cover. This picture is repeated and captioned on page 45 of the book. The front of the jacket has title and author in red ink; all other

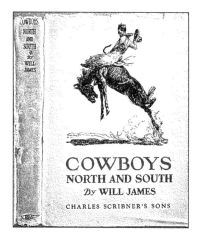

writing, front, back, foldovers, and spine, is in black ink. The front foldover has Scribner's description of the book, the rear one is promotion for *Scribner's Magazine.* The rear panel of the jacket lists 11 "important new books" and the list includes *Cowboys North and South.*

Pages: All text and captioned pages are numbered, starting with page 3 and ending at page 217. The front of the book has two free endpapers before the first title page, and at the rear, following page 217, there is one additional page with the Scribner's small logo centered on the page. Following that, there is one final free endpaper.

Illustrations: There are 57 fine separate b&w drawings, 59 drawings in all. (As stated above, two are repeated.) Fifty of the drawings are captioned, nine are untitled.

Story #1—COWBOYS NORTH AND SOUTH (The same title as the book.) Pages 3 - 26, with seven drawings.

The story details many variations in equipment, practices, and conditions that show how cowboying is done in different western states and climates.

Story #2 —BUCKING HORSES AND BUCKING HORSE RIDERS Pages 29 - 47, with seven drawings.

This story tells a lot about bucking horses and how and why they got that way: they are not normally trained by man to buck, but by environment and circumstance. Practice and experience can make a horse a better bucker. Practice is plumb necessary for good bucking riding also.

Story #3 — A COWPUNCHER SPEAKS
Pages 51 - 71, with eight drawings.

This story talks about the changes in the range lands, from the initial settlement by cattlemen to the first sheep, then homesteaders, then fences. The high prairies were very good for cattle country, but mighty hard on homesteaders. Then 'progress' got mighty hard on the cattle business too.

Story #4 — CATTLE RUSTLERS
Pages 75 - 100, with seven drawings.
Mostly about fairly small one-man operations. There is a good yarn here about one particular rustler that ends with an adequate moral.

Will finishes the chapter with a little vignette about a 'nester' (homesteader) killing a rancher's beef and the 'etiquette' required in that process.

Story #5 — WINTER MONTHS IN A COW CAMP
Pages 103 - 130, with six drawings.

This story is so true to life it could deter any young fellow from ever wanting to be a cowboy. Snow, cold, ice, long hours, and heavy, heavy work from before daylight till way after dark. One cow country dance and a wolf kill to break the monotony of a whole winter. This is cowboying as it actually is, but also at its **least** romantic.

Story #6 — THE MAKING OF A COW-HORSE
Pages 133 - 157, with six drawings.

A sharp contrast to story #5, this is the high and careful skill of breaking and making a top horse: taking a green and half-wild four-year-old and turning him from bronc to the best cow-savvy horse on the ranch.

Story #7 — THE LONGHORNS
> Pages 161 - 185, with six drawings.

> A very graphic tale of wild cattle handling.
> Roping them, running them, and all that goes
> with it.

Story #8 — PINION AND THE WILD ONES
> Pages 189 - 217, with four drawings.
> A wonderfully accurate, and all too short,
> story about wild mustangs and mustanging.
> Will James truly loved horses all his life, and
> he loved the wild ones most of all. Will's pre-
> occupation with and high regard for the wild

> mustang runs through many of his later books
> and stories, but is rarely done better than in
> this story that first appeared in *The Saturday
> Evening Post* in the May 19, 1924 issue.

7

Later Editions: The first Scribner's reprint was issued in 1925 and had the date 1925 at the bottom of the title page. The size, pagination, binding, and all other details were the same as in the first edition.

The second Scribner's reprint also was nearly identical to the first edition and has 1926 on the bottom of the title page. The obverse of the first half-title page has 'By Will James *Cowboys North and South* and *The Drifting Cowboy*' added. Both the 1925 and 1926 reprints were issued with a later-state dust jacket.

Later Scribner's reprints were all in smaller format.

Typical: 1931 on title page — 8-1/4" x 5-3/4", 217 pages.

1944 on title page — 8-1/4" x 5-3/4", 217 pages.

This title was also issued by Grosset & Dunlap; 8-1/4" x 5-3/4" by 1", still with 217 pages. None of the Grosset & Dunlap's bears any date on either the books or djs and we don't know how often they reprinted the Will James titles.

On these reprints G & D made at least three states of dust jackets, the back cover being different among the three states. All G & D Will James titles have *The Dark Horse* (first published in 1939) listed on the back of the jacket, hence all were produced after 1939.

The Drifting Cowboy
1925

Contents: Seven more wonderfully illustrated short stories with no single connecting character or theme, though all are narrated in the first person singular.

Comments: This second Will James book is also assembled from previously published short stories taken from about five different magazines. The book continues to teach the ways of the working and playing West. Will James shows the fun side and the rough side of the cowboy's life. As with his first book, this title is very scarce in a fine first edition with all the gilt lettering on the spine and with a fine dust jacket.

First Edition: *The Drifting Cowboy* was produced in only one first edition state and is identified as such by the date, 1925, at the bottom of the title page under the Scribner's name. All subsequent Scribner's reprints have a later date or no date at the bottom of the title page.

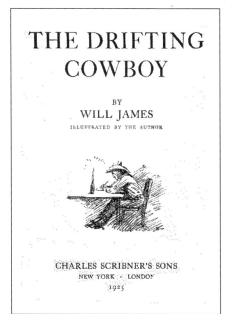

THE DRIFTING
COWBOY

BY
WILL JAMES
ILLUSTRATED BY THE AUTHOR

CHARLES SCRIBNER'S SONS
NEW YORK · LONDON
1925

Size & Price: 9-1/2" high, by 7-1/4" deep, by 1" thick. Price $3.50

Binding: Tan paper front and rear covers, with brown cloth on spine and wrapped around 1" onto both the tan paper covers.

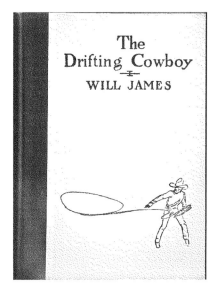

A fine line sketch on the front cover shows a cowboy throwing a 'front footing' loop. Front cover has title, author, and sketch printed in brown ink. The spine has title, author, and Scribners in gold lettering. The gold is usually all or partially flaked off, but a gray residual underlayer allows you to read the copy. This flaking of the gilt even occurs on some dust-jacketed copies, so books with the gilt in fine condition are few and far between.

Dust Jacket: The front cover of the tan paper jacket has a drawing of a mounted cowboy "on the drift" and leading a pack horse carrying his bedroll and 'possibles.' Title and author are on cover and spine, with Scribners at the bottom of the spine. The front foldover carries the Scribner's description of the book. The rear one has the same description of *Cowboys North and*

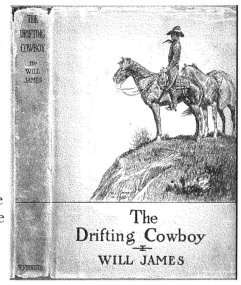

South as on the front foldover on that first title. The back of *The Drifting Cowboy* first edition dj has four 1924 reviews of *Cowboys North and South.*

Pages: All text and captioned drawing pages are numbered, 239 pages in all, starting at page 3 and ending at page 241. The first edition has one free endpaper at the front of the book and two at the back.

Illustrations: There are 44 titled drawings plus 14 untitled ones; all are b&w. The untitled picture on the Contents page is repeated at page 111.

Story #1 — ONCE A COWBOY

Pages 3 - 31, with six drawings about cowboys and cowboying.

The good and the bad in a cowboy's day. But, "Once a cowboy, always a cowboy."

Story #2 — FILLING IN THE
CRACKS
Pages 35-68,
with nine
drawings.
Cowboy
movie work
in Holly-
wood. Real
cowboys as
extras and
doubles for
the 'leading man.' This, and many other
Will James short stories, can be found in his
fact/fiction autobiography, *The Lone Cowboy*
(1930).

Story #3 — DESERT RANGE RIDING
Pages 71 - 99, with seven drawings.
Some of the rough and tedious end of
cowboying: 18-, 24-, and even 36-hour days
in all weathers, with hardly a break for man
or horse.

Story #4 — FIRST MONEY

Pages 103 - 134, with six drawings.

A good descriptive tale of the early days of small town rodeoing and the shenanigans that could be, and were, practiced by management and contestants alike.

Story #5 — WHEN WAGES ARE LOW

Pages 137 - 166, with nine fine drawings.

Another rambling tale about hard times, slim pickings, and simple pleasures in the cowboy year. There are four good descriptive pages on 'grub line' riding and the etiquette involved therein. The last few pages of this short story are a lovely vignette about the taking of 'the white wolf.'

Story #6 — A COWBOY IN THE MAKING
Pages 169 - 200, with seven drawings.
This is a tale that Will James tells in many
different ways in his later books and stories.
How a 'greenhorn towny' wants to be a cow-
boy.... Some make it and some don't.

Story #7 – HIS WATERLOO
Pages 203 - 241, with eight drawings.

This is a straight
bucking horse and
bronc riding tale
full of good
descriptions and
some of Will
James' best
bucking horse
drawings ever.

Later Editions: The first Scribner's reprint is 1926 with that date on the bottom of the title page; 9-1/2" by 7-1/4", 241 pages.

The next Scribner's reprint has 1929 on title page; 9-1/2" by 7-1/4", 241 pages.

The one after that has 1930 on title page; 9-1/2" by 7-1/4", 241 pages. All three of the above have same size and binding as the 1925 first edition; half brown cloth and tan paper.

A later Scribner's reprint, 1931, has smaller format and yellowish cloth binding; 1931 on title page; 8-3/8" by 6" by 1-1/8", 241 pages.

Another later Scribner's is a wartime reprint with 1945 on the title page; yellow cloth binding; 241 pages; 8-1/4" by 5-1/8", only 3/4" thick.

Grosset & Dunlap also reprinted this title, sometime after 1939; 8-1/4" by 5-5/8" by 1", 241 pages.

SMOKY
1926

Contents: Smoky is a novel about a western cowhorse, and mostly from that horse's own point of view. Starting with the day he is born and continuing with his colt and adolescent years, the main story line takes him through his first taste of being handled and ridden and on to his training into one of the top cow horses in five remudas. Smoky was a 'one man horse,' meaning that only Clint, the man who started him, could ride him. When Smoky was stolen he turned into an outlaw and then into a top bucking horse on the rodeo circuit. At the end of the story he is half starved and badly stove up. Smoky is about to be turned into chicken feed when Clint spots and rescues him. A mighty fine ending for all.

Comments: Smoky was certainly one of the very best of Will James' 24 books and the first printing of the first edition sold out before the ink was dry. In 1927 Smoky won the prestigious Newbery Medal. This accolade is awarded annually by the American Library Association for the year's most distinguished contribution to American literature for children. Smoky has been read by both young and old from its first airing in Scribner's Magazine in April of 1926 right on up to these present days over 70 years later.

A first edition, first printing Smoky is a rare bird; if in a first-state dust jacket, a treasure indeed.

First Edition: First published in four consecutive issues of *Scribner's Magazine*, April through July 1926, *Smoky* came out in book form in September of 1926 and was reprinted nine more times in 1926 alone.

The first book printing has 1926 at the bottom of the title page and only three lines of printing on the copyright page. All subsequent 1926 Scribner's reprint copyright pages have the reprint history starting with a fourth line on the second, third, and fourth printings, and after the fourth printing they have more than four lines.

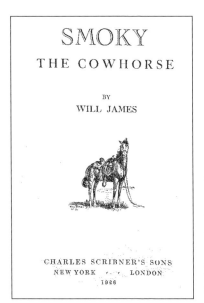

SMOKY

THE COWHORSE

BY
WILL JAMES

CHARLES SCRIBNER'S SONS
NEW YORK   LONDON
1926

There were ten American printings of *Smoky* in 1926, and five of those were in the Christmas month of December. After 1926, and including the Classic Edition, there have been too many reprints to reasonably count, certainly more than 40.

An interesting side note on the first editions and reprints of *Smoky* is that there is a glaring typographical error at the bottom of page 44, 'hou gt' in place of 'thought', and it carries through the whole first 11 reprints including the larger format 'Popular Edition' of August 1927.

The error is finally corrected in the 'New Popular Edition' later in 1927. Scribner's London branch also produced a U.K. first edition in 1926. It has tan covers and a wrap-around brown cloth spine. It is the same size, and produced from the same printing plates, probably in New York; also, the error on page 44 is present.

Size & Price: 8-1/4" high, by 6-1/8" deep, by 1-1/4" thick. Price: $2.50

Binding: Green cloth with title and author in black on front cover and spine, and with Scribner's in black at bottom of spine. At the center of the front cover under the author there is a nice line sketch in red ink of the bridled head of a cowhorse.

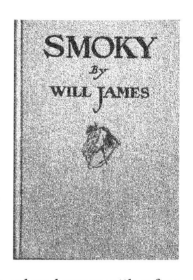

Dust Jacket: The dj is pale cream-colored paper with a fine black-and-white drawing on the front cover showing a saddled and bridled cowhorse standing 'ground-hitched' in front of a corral gate. This same sketch, much reduced in size and without the corral gate, appears on the title page of the book. The title at the top and author at the bottom of the jacket cover are in red ink. Title and author are at the top and Scribners at the bottom of the spine in black ink. At the fourth printing of the book, Scribner's added the words "Fourth Printing" in red ink in the middle of the spine of the dj. The following eight printings had the printing history on the spine. The front foldover of the jacket has the price, $2.50, and Scribner's

18

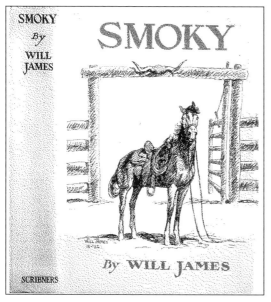

description of the book. The rear one has a pair of reviews of Will James' first two books. The rear cover of the *Smoky* dj has the fine portrait drawing by Bert Sharkey of Will James from the shoulders up and with an unusual bow tie and the usual big hat.

Pages: All text pages are numbered and the full-page-drawing pages use a number, though it does not always appear on the page. The book starts at Chapter One, page 1, and ends at page 310. The first edition has one free endpaper at the front and one at the back of the book.

Illustrations: In and on the book there are 46 b&w illustrations in addition to the jacket ones; 43 are titled. A cropped version of the jacket picture is on the title page. The sketch on the second title page is repeated and titled on page 103.

Later editions: After the first 11 printings of the first edition, Scribner's produced a larger book under the "Popular Edition" label in August 1927, 9-1/8" by 7", still 310 pages, and using the same page-printing plates with the same error on page 44. Also in August 1927 Scribner's produced a "New Popular Edition" in a smaller green cloth format, 7-5/8" by 5-1/2", still 310 pages, but finally with the error corrected. This new edition also was reprinted in November 1927, about the same, but with tan cloth binding. Scribner's continued to publish *Smoky* in 1928, 1930, and so on.

In 1932 Scribner's came out with a five-book set in three states and called it The Drifting Cowboy Series (only so named on the dust wrappers): *Smoky, Sand, Lone Cowboy, Sun Up,* and *Big Enough.* The three states are: (1) all green cloth binding with gold lettering, (2) the same but with red background under spine lettering; (3) a tan cloth with brown lettering. All are 8-3/8" by 6" deep.

In 1937 Scribner's produced the identical five-book Drifting Cowboy Series in the same three states and *with the same djs.* After 1937 Scribner's is not known to have produced the **complete** *Smoky* with all of the original illustrations. Scribner's produced and reproduced the 'Smoky Illustrated Classic' edition starting in 1929 (see 6th book chapter here).

Other publishers also produced this title. First, A.L. Burt published "The complete novel from which the Fox photoplay was produced" — this version had only 43 pictures of the 46 in the first edition. Also the dj picture is **not** by Will James even though he was available then. 7-3/4" by 5-3/8", pale orange cloth binding.

Grosset & Dunlap reprinted *Smoky* at least four times with four different back covers of the dj — All G&D Will James reprints were published after 1939 and all G&D Will James djs were illustrated with crude and garish color copies, by others, of Will James drawings.

A very important point — **never** buy a Grosset & Dunlap *Smoky* reprint if you want the book as produced. G&D has the following on the front foldover of some of the reprint jackets:

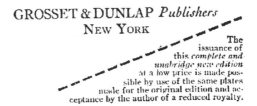

GROSSET & DUNLAP *Publishers*
NEW YORK

The issuance of this *complete and unabridged new edition* at a low price is made possible by use of the same plates made for the original edition and acceptance by the author of a reduced royalty.

Actually almost nothing is the same. The pagination is entirely different and all of the G&D *Smoky* reprints are illustrated entirely with drawings from other Will James books. **None** of the drawings illustrates the text. It's an inexplicable omission/substitution.

G&D reprints of Will James' other books used some of the original drawings, although not usually all of them, and they were often so poorly reproduced that that was criminal too.

Cow Country
1927

Contents: This is another group of short stories. They were all also published in magazines first, then gathered here by Scribner's for this great book.

Comments: This is Will James' third book of short stories. There are eight of them, and all are dandies. The book is very frequently overlooked by even his most enthusiastic fans. It was only reprinted a few times by Scribner's, and only reprint publisher Grosset & Dunlap brought out an (inferior) edition in later years. Certainly the stories are excellent examples of his talent, and the simple two-page preface is a beautifully concise statement of what Will almost religiously believed. To top it off, this book has some of his very finest drawings. Almost every drawing in the book shows Will James at the very top of his skill. Ask yourself if there is any equine artist, past or present, who could tell this picture story better or more graphically, even in full color, than Will has done here on page 185 in black and white.

First Edition: The first edition has 1927 at the bottom of the title page and six lines of type on the copyright page headed by: "Copyright, 1927 BY". A widely used and usually reliable reference is Ramon Adams, "The Rampaging Herd," but he erroneously cites *Cowboys North and South* '24, *Drifting Cowboy* '25, and *Cow Country* '27 as having the Scribner's 'A' on the first-edition copyright page. T'ain't so fellas.... Scribner's didn't start using the A until late 1929.

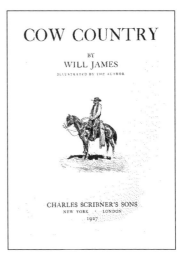

Size & Price: 9-1/2" high, by 7-3/8" deep, by 1" thick. Price $3.50

Binding: Deep red cloth binding with title and author on the front cover and spine. Scribners is at the bottom of the spine and there is a fine sketch of a longhorn steer skull and coiled rope on the front cover. All the lettering and the sketch are in black ink.

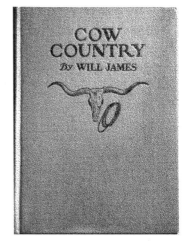

Dust Jacket: A lovely cream-white paper jacket with a fine picture of an old cowman sitting on a nicely set-up horse printed in black. Title and author are in blue on the front cover; and in black on the spine with Scribners at the bottom. The rear of the jacket is devoted to the first three Will James books with review notes and quotes on each. The rear foldover promotes *The Cowboy* by Philip Rollins, and the front foldover has Scribner's promotion for this book, as usual.

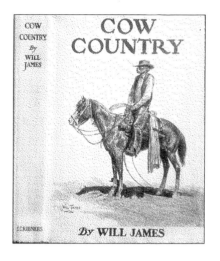

Pages: The pages are numbered from 3 to 242. The first edition has one free endpaper at the front of the book and two at the back.

Illustrations: There are 40 b&w drawings in *Cow Country* including one on the cover; 28 are with title captions. Of the untitled drawings, several appear more than once. The first title page drawing includes the sketch on the front cover. The title-page sketch is a much reduced copy of the full-page drawing on page 83 of the book, the same drawing that is on the front of the dust jacket. The Contents page sketch is taken from the lovely full-page drawing on page 5.

Story #1 — THE WILD HORSE

Pages 3 - 31, with five drawings including the one at the story's title page.

The story is about the sad problems brought on by too many wild horses for the range to support. It graphically describes some of the bad side of catching the wild  ones, and it doesn't offer much in the way of solutions. (The Wild Horse Annie Act of Congress in 1972 made a start and the Bureau of Land Management is finally beginning to get a handle on the problem 70 years after this story was written.)

Story #2 — WHEN IN ROME

Pages 35 - 64, with five drawings.

 The story is a tongue-in-cheek description of the Eastern way of riding and working compared with the Western. A simple well-told tale.

Story #3 — MONTY OF THE "Y" BENCH
        Pages 67 - 98, with five drawings.

      This is a sort of second chapter to story #2.
It tends to complete the circle.

Story #4 — SILVER MOUNTED
        Pages 101 - 124, with three drawings.

      A good rodeo rider who learned bronc riding,
roping, and cowboying only in the arena, tries
his hand at being a real working cowboy out
on the range. "It's not the same thing,
Charlie."

Story #5 — THE LAST CATCH

Pages 127 - 137, with three drawings and one of those is an example of Will's exaggerated, wild horse drawings.

This drawing on page 129 shows the wild mustang stud as he looks to a cowboy, way up there on high ground above you, preening, because he knows he's got the high bulge on you. He looks like a thousand-dollar horse in a hundred-dollar market. Of course if you later get the bulge on him and catch him, a close look at him in your corral with his preening and liberty gone can sure make you wonder what it was you saw in him way up on that high ridge. But turn him loose, like in the sketch at the start of this chapter, and he'll sure give you that 'look of eagles' over both shoulders as he makes tracks far apart heading back to his home range and harem.

Story #6 — TWO OLD TIMERS
Pages 141 - 176, with five drawings.

Quite a deep philosophical tale about change. Change in time, change in people, and change in the range. Will James was only in his early 30s when he wrote this. It shows a lot about the depth of observation that Will had. The story could be as true today as it was in the 1920s. The range lands have seen a lot of abuse in the last 150 years but at least parts of them are making a real comeback today. Also, the changes in ranching are getting more pronounced each decade.

Story #7— COMPLETE
Pages 179 - 215, with five drawings.

Another case of Will James' philosophizing; a bit idealistic perhaps, but a good story anyway. It has a nice little vignette on how a cowboy grows from roaming to ranching. Many details are amazingly contemporary and equally possible today, over three generations later.

Story #8 — THE BREED OF 'EM
Pages 219 - 242, with four drawings.

About a ranch/range cowboy's work ethic and work hours. Quoting the field foreman: "He'll ride horses I wouldn't touch with a forty-foot pole, in all kinds of weather.... *but he won't work.*"

Later Editions: The first-edition second printing is nearly identical with the first issue. It has 1927 at the bottom of the title page, same rust red cloth, same size, same copyright page. But, there is a small capital letter 'B' under the six lines of type on the copyright page.

Because of the tremendous success of *Smoky* in 1926, Scribner's printed a larger than usual first two runs. This book did not sell like *Smoky*, though, and I find no other re-prints of *Cow Country* by Scribner's or anyone else until 1945 and beyond.

In the 1945 war year Scribner's reprinted a small copy in greenish-gray cloth covers, 8-3/8" by 5-7/8" and only half as thick, still 242 pages though.

Grosset & Dunlap reprinted *Cow Country* at least three times with three slightly different states of djs. Again the dj art was by some G&D house artist — obviously nothing like Will James' standards.

SAND
1929

Contents: Sand is a novel about a wastrel tenderfoot who turns himself into a working cowboy. It takes a few years but he gets the job done. He gets the champion mustang nobody could catch, and the gal that was even harder to corral. A very satisfactory conclusion.

Comments: Will James had very high hopes for this book and worked mighty hard on it for most of two years. The drawings rank up with his best and none is a repeat from his first four books, a practice that became common in some of his later writings. The critics had raved about his books one after the other so perhaps they were afraid to keep saying only nice things forever. Some of them still liked his output, but a few called this book a letdown from his previous work and weak in plot. Myself, I like Horatio Alger plots and mustang stories. I loved this book.

First Edition: Sand was printed in two first editions concur-

SAND

BY
WILL JAMES

CHARLES SCRIBNER'S SONS
NEW YORK · LONDON
1929

rently by Scribner's in New York and in London, in 1929. If the 1929 date appears at the bottom of the title page and there are only three lines of print on the copyright page, the book is the first edition. The American first has New York - London under Scribner's name and the U.K. first has London only, above Scribner's name.

Size & Price: 8-1/4" high, by 6" deep, by 1-1/4" thick. Price $2.50

Binding: The regular first edition is bound in green cloth with black ink title and author on front cover and spine and Scribners printed in black at the bottom of the spine. There is a very nice picture of a standing cowboy in chaps also printed in black ink on the lower right-hand corner of the front cover. The front cover has a broad 1/8th-inch red line under the title.

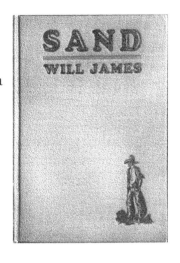

Dust Jacket: Light tan paper jacket with a wonderful black ink drawing of a majestic wild horse triumphantly outrunning a hotly pursuing cowboy who is futilely trying to rope him. This front cover picture is an example of the very best of Will James' talent as an artist and illustrator. Title and one line of copy are on the front panel in red, and above the title there is a red line that wraps around onto the spine. The author is above that line in black on the cover. All the printing on the

spine is black with the title over the red line, author under it, and Scribners at the bottom. The front foldover has the Scribner's blurb about the book, the rear foldover a pitch for the four preceding Will James books, with quotes from reviews of *Smoky*. The rear of the jacket has a small drawing from page 1 of the book at the top, and then "A word from the author."

Pages: This book starts on page 1 with "A First Word," which runs two pages and three paragraphs. The first and last paragraphs are the same as those on the back panel of the dust jacket. The story starts at Chapter One, page 3, and finishes on page 328. There is one free endpaper at the front of the book and one at the back.

Illustrations: The one very wonderful black-and-white drawing on the dj is not repeated in the book, so if you want all 48 of the separate Will James drawings and sketches in *Sand* you have to get the first edition in dj. All told there are 47 separate drawings in and on the book itself. The title page sketch is repeated, in slightly less detail, on the front cover of the book.

Later Editions: After the first edition of *Sand* came out in 1929 there was no second Scribner's printing until an almost identical reprint came out with 1932 at the bottom of the title page. Also in 1932, *Sand* was included in the five-book sets that came out first in three states in 1932, and then again in 1937. (See the details in the *Smoky* chapter.) Even though Scribner's started using the distinctive Scribner's letter 'A' under the copyright for other first editions later in 1929, it never appeared in the first edition of *Sand*.

In 1943 Scribner's came out with an edition that is almost identical to the first edition: same size, same green cloth binding, 328 pages, etc. But it has 1943 at the bottom of the title page and 6 lines of type on the copyright page. This was right in the middle of the World War II paper shortage, when most Scribner's reprints of Will James books, and others, were reduced in size and thickness. This 1943 *Sand* reprint was not reduced in any way.

Blue Ribbon Books produced a reprint with orange covers the same size as the Scribner's first edition. Date is unknown.

Sun Dial Press in 1941: Same size, with salmon boards.

A.L. Burt about 1931: 7-5/8" by 5-3/8" by 1-3/8", with two cover states, gray-green and green.

Grosset & Dunlap reprinted *Sand* with at least three different dj states (all three djs with the crummy house artist touch-up of the original Will James first-edition dj cover picture).

SMOKY

ILLUSTRATED CLASSIC EDITION

1929

Contents: This edition has the same text as the first edition. The dust jacket, binding, size and pictures are different; see below.

Comments: Although a most beautiful appearing book, the Classic Edition is a travesty in that it leaves out 82% of Will's line drawings that so wonderfully illustrate the text in the first edition. To read and appreciate *Smoky* as Will James produced it in the Newbery-award-winning version, you must read any one of the 15 or so Scribner's *Smoky* printings produced from 1926 through 1928. Scribner's put out a few later editions of the original work, but by far most of the reprints they produced in later decades were of the emasculated 'Classics' version of the book.

The Classic is the same story as the original, and, while Will James was a great writer of horse and cow country stories, his unique talent was as <u>both</u> author <u>and</u> illustrator. In my personal opinion, he was one of the two outstandingly best 'horses in action' illustrators in the entire 20th century (the other was Paul Brown).

Will James' great gift was the telling of stories in words <u>and</u> pictures. Frequently, "A picture is worth a thousand words."

First Issue: The first issue of the Illustrated Classic was published after *Sand* in 1929. It is about impossible to identify if you only look at the copyright page. In point of fact, in the first dozen years that Scribner's republished this edition, only one page differs from the original. Fortunately that one page is always different right up to 1942. The one different page faces the title page. If it lists the first five Will James books with *Sand* at the top of the list, the book so blessed is the 1929 first of the Classic edition.

Size & Price: 9-1/2" high by 7-1/2" deep by 1-1/8" thick. Price: $2.50

Binding: Scribner's started The Scribner's Illustrated Classics Series early in this century. They continued to produce them through the 1960s as far as I know, and probably beyond. From inception through the 1940s, they produced dozens of titles all the same size and format, with black cloth bindings, a full-size colored illustration on the front cover, and a double-spread colored illustration on the front and rear paste-downs and adjacent endpapers. The *Smoky* Classic first issue has the standard black cloth binding with a full-page colored illustration of a cowboy rolling a smoke and standing beside his saddled pony. The pony is Smoky, as described and pictured

elsewhere in the book. The title is at the top of the picture and the author at the bottom; both are in black ink. The spine has the title at the top, 'Illustrated by the author' in the middle, and Scribners at the bottom. All the spine printing is in gold.

Dust Jacket: The first-issue dj is rare and different from all of the reprint jackets that followed. The 'first' is printed on light tan paper and the fine full-color front cover picture is from page 208 of the book. The book title is over the picture, and author and publisher are under it. All are in black ink, as is the spine printing, which is a repeat of that which is on the spine of the book. The front and rear foldovers are pitches for other Scribner's titles and the rear panel lists 32 other Illustrated Classic titles.

Pages: In this edition the actual pages are larger, which gets a few more words on each page. Also there are fewer illustrations. The text pages are numbered from page 3 to page 263. The color-plate illustrations are not numbered. There are no free endpapers, front or back.

Illustrations: This is the first Will James book with colored illustrations. Counting the front cover, the endpapers, the title page, and those in the text, there are nine new colored pictures in this edition that are not in the first edition. **BUT** .... where the first edition had a total of 45 fine b&w illustrations in the text, the Classic Edition has **only eight** of them! That's 37 wonderful Will James illustrations, all of which illustrated and enhanced the text, that the Classic reader doesn't get to see. There is no way that nine colored pages (only six of which are in the text) can improve the story line enough to make up for that criminal omission.

Later Editions: The first reprint of the 1929 Classic that I have seen has *Sun Up* at the top of the book list opposite the title page and the second has *Big Enough* above that. Both those books came out in 1931, with *Sun Up* first. This clearly indicates that the Classic was re-printed at least twice in 1931. Other reprints have books that were written after 1931 at the top of the list. By far the greatest number of reprints have *The American Cowboy* at the top, showing that they were produced in, or, even more frequently, after 1942. Up until at least 1942 all have exactly the same copyright page as the first issue in 1929!

A 1933 edition was published, and in 1935 Scribner's issued the first boxed edition that we know about. I have seen one Scribner's box with the first-state dj picture on it, but I have no date of reference to go with that box. The 1935 box (and all others I have seen) has the second-state dj and front cover picture on the box cover. The 1937 edition was also boxed, and perhaps others were too.

By 1965 Scribner's was issuing the *Smoky* Classic with plain salmon-colored cover and endpapers — no picture, but still with the old cover picture on the darker salmon djs.

Scribner's Illustrated Classic reprint editions were only done by Scribner's. The Classics were never licensed to others.

LONE COWBOY
1930

Contents: This book is titled "An autobiography." In actual fact, all the details here of Will James' life up until his mid-teens are entirely fiction and the rest of the book is a nice balance between biography and fiction. I call it a wonderful 'fictionography.'

Comments: This is certainly one of Will James best and most wanted books. There were a great many of them printed and sold in the 1930 first year, and a very great many of them printed and sold since. The green cloth cover first edition was chosen as a Book of the Month Club selection (BOMC) and was also sold in 1930 through the standard retail channels and stores. The book was released for sale on August 1, 1930, and copies were sent to book reviewers somewhat before that date. The books for BOMC and those for the trade were the same; there is no BOMC notification printed in the books.

So why four states of the first edition dj? My personal speculation is that the BOMC copies were released with the orange jacket, the *N.Y. Herald Tribune* quote, and the $2.75 price. We know from the review copy that the trade copies were released with the green jacket, the *Tribune* quote, and the $2.75 price. And we believe that the U.K. copies in blue covers were offered with orange jackets, *The Daily News* (London) quote, and no price on the jacket. The above speculations offer a plausible distribution of three of the jackets.

What about the priced green jacket with the *Daily News* quote ??? Come on you readers, give me a hand, tell me what you think.

The green cloth first with an 'A' is by far the most common first edition Will James book — with or without dj. So while I'm speculating, let's do some more guessing.

Smoky was first introduced in September of 1926. It was reprinted nine times more before that year ended. The reprints were all the same and from the same plates, with only one exception: the copyright page faithfully recorded each and every reprint. But 1930 was a depression year; I know from experience that publishers did a number of things in those tough years that they never did before or since. My personal speculation is that Scribner's kept printing and binding *Lone Cowboy* as demand dictated right through that year till Christmas, and did not choose to give those ongoing printings a mention on the copyright page as they had done with *Smoky*.

First Edition: *Lone Cowboy* has its first edition in three states, all three with the Scribner's 'A'. All came out in 1930 with 1930 under Scribner's name at the bottom of the title page. The limited edition of 250 came out last. The first state is the well known green cloth binding edition. The second state is the

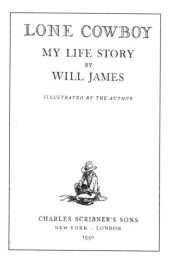

LONE COWBOY

MY LIFE STORY
BY
WILL JAMES

ILLUSTRATED BY THE AUTHOR

CHARLES SCRIBNER'S SONS
NEW YORK · LONDON
1930

Scribner's London, U.K. edition. The third state is the limited edition, 250 copies, each with a different original full-page ink drawing signed: Will James '30.

Size & Price: 8-1/2" high, by 6-1/8" deep, and 1-5/8" thick. All three first editions are the same size, although condition can make the exact measurements vary slightly. The standard American first edition was priced at $2.75. I don't know the price of the limited or the London editions.

Binding: The regular first edition is bound in forest green cloth with gold lettered title and author on cover and top of spine and Scribners at the bottom as usual. There is a black printed line

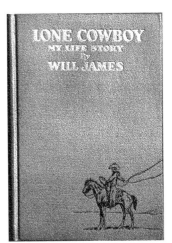

sketch of a mounted cowboy swinging his riata in the lower right-hand corner of the front cover. The London first edition is bound in solid blue cloth with gold printing. The front cover has title at the top and author at the bottom, and the spine has title and author at the top with Scribners at the bottom.

The limited edition is covered in pale green cloth with a deep tan cloth spine wrapped 1/2" over front and rear covers. Both front and rear covers are plain with no markings. The top third of the spine is covered with a brown leather label that has a thin double ruled line 1/8" in from the edges, with title and author inside the lines. The lines and printing are in gold. This limited edition was issued in a slipcase covered in pale green paper. The slipcase spine has a larger brown leather label with the thin double lines at top and bottom only. At the top it has title and author, a single line, "Limited edition," a single line, and then at the bottom "With one original drawing by the author." Again the lines and printing are in gold on the brown leather label.

Dust Jacket: The first edition was issued with four distinctly different printed djs, two in green and two in orange, both printed on a pale cream-colored paper. It is my very strong opinion that the first state of the first-edition dj is the green jacket with the *New York Herald Tribune* review quotation at the bottom of the rear dj foldover. This belief is supported by a copy of a fine first with a jacket of the above description that I acquired over 20 years ago from a Boston dealer who had just bought a lot of fine firsts from the estate of a newspaper book reviewer. That copy of *Lone Cowboy* in the described dust jacket still had the Scribner's "review notice to the literary editor" tipped into the book and is in my personal collection.

The other green jacket also appears with all details the same, except the review quotations at the top and bottom of the rear foldover are quotes from *The Aberdeen Press* (Aberdeen) and *The Daily News* (London), replacing quotes from *The Boston Herald* (Boston) and the *New York Herald Tribune* (New York). The orange jackets also come with those two states of review quotes.

WILL JAMES

has also written and illustrated

Sand

"*With picture and text Will James has brought the ranch country to life.*"
—*Boston Herald.*

Cow Country

"*A panorama of the Western ranges as vivid and realistic as the country itself.*"
—*Philadelphia Ledger.*

Smoky

"*Will James has done the 'Black Beauty' of the cow country.*"—*New York Times.*

The Drifting Cowboy

"*We could read it and look at the drawings all night.*"
—*The New Yorker.*

Cowboys, North and South

"*A gorgeous and almost unbelievable book in which the rider of the range, rid of sentimental misinterpretation, speaks for himself.*"—*New York Herald Tribune.*

WILL JAMES

has also written and illustrated

Sand

"*Mr. James has built up one of the greatest pony yarns ever penned.*"—*Aberdeen Press.*

Cow Country

"*A panorama of the Western ranges as vivid and realistic as the country itself.*"
—*Philadelphia Ledger.*

Smoky

"*Will James has done the 'Black Beauty' of the cow country.*"—*New York Times.*

The Drifting Cowboy

"*We could read it and look at the drawings all night.*"
—*The New Yorker.*

Cowboys, North and South

"*His book gives a vivid picture of the sensational everyday life of the prairie.*"
—*Daily News (London).*

All four states of the djs have a tinted portrait of Will on the front cover. The title and 'MY LIFE STORY' is printed over the picture, and author under it. The spine has the title at the top, then author, then a silhouette sketch of a mounted cowboy riding down a steep pitch, then Scribners at the bottom. On the green djs all the lettering and the silhouette sketch are in white. The orange ones have those same details in green on the orange. The several U.K. blue cloth editions that I have seen in djs have all been in the orange jackets and the price is omitted at the top of the front foldover.

The limited edition was not issued in a dj; it came in a slipcase as described above.

Pages: All three firsts - standard, U.K., and Limited - start at Chapter One, page 1, and end at page 431. All have one free endpaper at the front and two at the back of the book. It is my observation that all three editions were printed from the same plates on pretty much the same paper, though an expert on those details may give me an argument on that point.

The limited edition has a limitation message on the front of the first printed page and eliminates the book list from the back of that page that is included in the other two editions. After the limitation page, the limited edition has a fine original ink drawing, signed by the author and on a slightly better grade of paper. The other two editions do not have that extra page, of course.

A typical signed ink drawing.
There were 250, all different.

Illustrations: All three editions have all the same illustrations between the covers, excepting the signed original drawing in the limited. The limited does not have the front cover sketch the other two editions have. Also, it doesn't have the dj so it doesn't have the tinted portrait thereon.

The limited does have the frontispiece photo portrait, and the back of the dust jacket sketch is repeated after page 431 of the book, so it has that one too. With those exceptions, all are illustrated with one photo portrait, 35 titled drawings, and 36 sketches not separately titled, for a total of 71 individual drawings inside the book, plus one on the cover.

Later Editions: The first Scribner's reprint of *Lone Cowboy* was done in 1931 and is the same size and with the same green cloth, gold printed covers as the first edition. It has 1931 at bottom of title page and no Scribner's 'A' on copyright page. The reprint is far more rare than the first edition — and more dear too. The second Scribner's reprint was included as part of the five-book three-state Drifting Cowboy Series in 1932 and 1937 (see that description in the *Smoky* chapter). Also in 1932, Scribner's produced the first Illustrated Classic edition of *Lone Cowboy* with 36 additional color and b&w illustrations. Scribner's almost never thereafter reprinted *Lone Cowboy* in the original first-edition state, although they did do at least one reprint in 1946 with a blue cloth cover and the same 431 pages. They did continue to reprint the Classic edition through the 1960s and probably beyond.

No other publisher has reprinted this work until recently.

Sun Up
1931

Contents: There are 16 fully illustrated Will James short stories in this book and they are all examples of his very best writings and illustrations.

Comments: Sun Up is the first of Will James' books to reuse stories that were already used in previous books. Of the 16 stories 9 are reprinted from previous Will James books: three from *Cowboys North and South,* three from *Drifting Cowboy,* and three from *Cow Country.*

When friends ask me for one of Will James books as a 'get acquainted' read, I very frequently suggest *Sun Up* for a starter.

First Edition: Sun Up was published in two very different first-edition states at the same time, and both have the Scribner's 'A'. The first state is the black cloth book with a fine colored picture of a bucking horse and rider on the front cover.

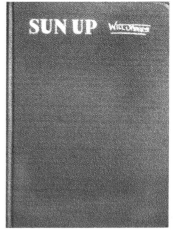

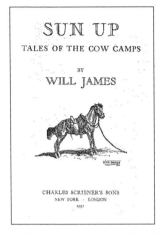
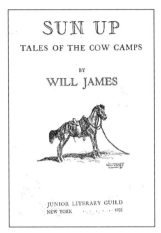

It looks very much like the popular Scribner's Illustrated Classic Series but it is not one of them. Among other things it is smaller in size.

The other state of the *Sun Up* first edition is The Junior Literary Guild edition, which has a solid cloth cover and no front cover picture. Both editions are identical in all details except for the cover and title page.

Size & Price: Both editions are 9" high, by 7" deep, by 1-3/8" thick. The individual price of Scribner's black cloth edition was $2.50. The Junior Literary Guild book was presumably a subscription offering. The price is not stated on the dj front foldover.

Binding: The first state has black cloth covers and spine with a full size color picture on the front cover; title and author are in blue ink at the bottom of the picture. Printed in gold on the spine, title and author are at the top with a small cowboy hat between them, 'Illustrated by Author' in the middle, and Scribners at the bottom.

The second state has a red cloth binding and gold printing. The title and author are at the top of the front cover and the spine has the same printing as the first state including the hat.

Dust Jacket: It is my long-held position that the first-state *Sun Up* was never issued with a dust jacket. A later edition was issued in a box with the color picture that is on the cover of the book

reproduced on the cover of the box, but neither I nor any of my knowledgeable friends has ever seen a dj for the first state.

The second-state Junior Literary Guild book was issued with a dj. It is white paper with the fine color picture and printing from the first-state book cover on the front. Printed in black ink on the spine is title and author at the top, no hat, and at the bottom of the spine it says Junior Literary Guild. This second-state first edition dj is a rare bird and I've only seen about three or four of them in all my years.

Pages: There are 242 pages of text and pictures in *Sun Up,* starting at page 1 and finishing at page 242. In both states there is one free endpaper at the front of the book and one at the back.

Illustrations: The color picture on the front cover of the first state of *Sun Up* is the first use of color in a first-edition Will James book. You might bring up the *Smoky* Classic of 1929 but remember,

50

that was not a first edition. *Sun Up* is also the first 'first edition' to use many of the pictures that appeared in earlier books. Nevertheless, it has 79 b&w drawings and only *Cow Country* before it had more. The two action sketches in Will's Preface, as well as his words, are worth more than a second look. One more detail: this book has no 'list of illustrations' even though many are a full page and most are titled.

Story #1 — "HIS SPURS"

Pages 1 - 25, with five drawings. A nice tight rodeoing story about a ranching youngster of 15 or so growing into manhood, 'winning his spurs' literally and figuratively, and becoming a champion rodeo bronc rider.

Story #2 — ON THE DODGE

Pages 26 - 47, with three drawings.
An atypical yarn of a type similar to ones Will illustrated occasionally for pulp Westerns in his early artist years. Not a very good example of Will James' talents but amusing enough for a short read.

Story #3 —THE MAKING OF A COW-HORSE
    Pages 48 - 65, with six fine drawings.

First in *Cowboys North & South*, 1924, this
story is classic Will James at his very best,
describing the high and careful skill of breaking and making a top horse, starting with a
green and half-wild four-year-old and turning
him from a bronc into *"the top cow-horse in
four remudas."*

Story #4 — THE YOUNG COWBOY
    Pages 66 - 86, with five drawings.

Some of the details of this story were later
incorporated into the 1935 title *Young
Cowboy,* but this is a stand-alone episode
that illustrates what trying to be a man is like
for a ten-year-old cowboy kid. I was nowhere
near as tough as this young Billy, but I sure
took some of those same hard knocks.

Story #5 — CATTLE RUSTLERS

Pages 87 - 104, with seven drawings. Again, this title and story appeared first in *Cowboys North & South*, 1924. Mostly about fairly small one-man operations. There is a good yarn here about one particular rustler, that ends with an adequate moral. Will finishes the chapter with a little vignette about a 'nester' killing a rancher's beef and the good vs. bad manners of that process.

Story #6 — MIDNIGHT

Pages 105 - 124, with three drawings.

A wonderful mustanging story, it really shows Will's pride in and love of the wild horse and the wild horse country. Will James could always capture in words and pictures the wild horse as a cowboy sees him. Look at the picture on page 271 in this book, and I quote from page 111: "He left me and the corral seemed like without touching the earth, floating out a ways then turned and stood on his tiptoes, shook his head at me, let out a long whistle the same as to say 'this is sure a surprise' and away he went."

Story #7 — FIRST MONEY
Pages 125 - 147, with six drawings.

A good descriptive story about the early days of small town rodeoing and the she-nanigans that could be, and were, practiced by management and contestants alike. This story also appeared in *Drifting Cowboy.*

Story #8 — BUCKING HORSES AND BUCKING HORSE RIDERS
Pages 148 - 160, with seven drawings.

This is the third and last story in *Sun Up* from *Cowboys North & South.* This story tells a lot about bucking horses and how and why they got that way. They are not normally trained by man to buck, but by environment and circum-stance. Practice and experience makes for better bucking too. Practice is plumb necessary for good bucking riding.

Story #9 — HIS WATERLOO.

A repeat of the same story in *Drifting Cowboy.*
Pages 161 - 189, with only six drawings, two fewer than were in the *Drifting Cowboy* version.

This is a straight bucking horse and bronc riding tale, with a very graphic outline of how age can erode a bronc rider's skills.

Story #10 — "JAKE ADAMS, SOURDOUGH"
Pages 190 - 216, with three drawings.

A grand little people story that 'town folks'
may have trouble appreciating. But I've seen
a few of these independent old hermits way
away from anywhere and Will sure tells it
like it is.

Story #11 — A HOME GUARD
Pages 217 - 239, with three drawings.

This is a yarn about the making of a man
from a spoiled boy. A lot of horse work, and
horse sense in it too. They do play rough on a
working ranch. I had plenty of chance to
experience that myself.

Story #12 — FILLING IN THE CRACKS

The third story repeated from *Drifting Cowboy.* Pages 240 - 264, with only eight of the original nine drawings.

About cowboy movie work in Hollywood. Real cowboys as extras and doubles for the 'leading man.' This story is included, with many of his others, in his fact/fiction autobiography, *The Lone Cowboy.*

Story #13 — THE LAST CATCH

Pages 265 - 271 with only two drawings, and first printed in *Cow Country* in 1927.

For some reason Scribner's left out of this *Sun Up* story reprint the wonderful drawing on page 129 of the *Cow Country* version that I described and commented on at some considerable length in the foregoing chapter on that book. The grand and sentimental mustanging story text is all there but

why they left out that picture I'll never know.
Will James first did that illustration for a
story in the May 5th 1927 issue of *The
Youth's Companion* magazine. That story,
'The King' by E. E. Harriman, was totally a
different story and with different illustrations
by Will James, but the magazine put that
magnificent Will James 'mustang stud on
high ground' picture in vivid color on its front
cover, and that issue of the magazine has
been a collectors' item ever since.

Story #14 — "CUPID, THE MUSTANG"
Pages 272 - 301, with three drawings.

Will James almost never messes with that
'love stuff' and if he does touch on 'a hanker-
ing' little ever comes of it in his short stories.
This, however, is a simple little love story and
the only one I can remember of his scores of
stories where the love interest isn't secondary
in the plot.

Story #15 — SILVER MOUNTED
> Pages 302 - 320, with three pictures.

Another story taken from the book *Cow Country* and this one at least has all three of the same illustrations. A good rodeo rider who learned bronc riding, roping, and cowboying only in the arena tries his hand at being a real working cowboy out on the range. Many mighty good cowboys can't rodeo for beans. And quite a few top rodeo performers can be near useless on a working ranch. I've seen both kinds.

Story #16 — WHEN IN ROME
> Pages 321 - 342, with only four of the eight drawings that were in the original *Cow Country* version.

This one is a tongue-in-cheek comparison of the Eastern way of riding and working compared with the Western. A simple well-told tale.

Later Editions: A Scribner's second printing of the black cover state came out in 1931 and is exactly the same as the first edition, first state, except without the first-edition Scribner's 'A'. It was again reprinted the same way in 1932 with the date at bottom of the title page, and no 'A'. And it was done that way in 1934 and 1936 and probably other years as well.

Also in 1932 it was included with the Scribner's five-book, three-state Drifting Cowboy Series, repeated in 1937. (See *Smoky* chapter for that description.)

Grosset & Dunlap reprinted *Sun Up* at least three times after 1939.

BIG ENOUGH
1931

Contents: This is Will James' fourth novel and a choice one for young and older.

Comments: *Big Enough* is my favorite Will James book. It was given to me in my seventh year when it came out in 1931. It was my first Will James book of any kind and I identified with Little Billy, 'big enough' as soon as he could walk and ride. I also was always either too young or too small, or both, for doing all of the full size cowboying I wanted to do.

As stated elsewhere in this bibliography, Will James was first and last a story-teller and in this novel, as in most of his, wonderful little vignettes have been dropped in that can easily be pulled out to stand alone. This was done in some later Will James short story books, with stories pulled from *Lone Cowboy, Smoky,* and so forth.

First Edition: Big Enough was published in one single first-edition state and it has 1931 at the bottom of the title page and the all-important Scribner's 'A' under the copy-right.

BIG~ENOUGH
BY
WILL JAMES
ILLUSTRATED BY THE AUTHOR

CHARLES SCRIBNER'S SONS
NEW YORK · LONDON
1931

Size & Price: 8-1/2" high, by 6" deep, by 1-1/4" thick. Price $2.50

Binding: The first edition is bound in canary yellow cloth, and has a line sketch of two horses in the bottom right-hand corner of the front cover done in reddish brown ink. The front cover has the title and author in black ink and the spine has title and author at the top and Scribners at the bottom, all in black ink.

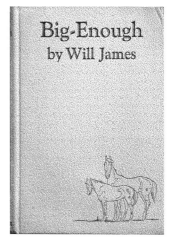

Dust Jacket: This book has a dust jacket of beige paper with a fine picture in color of a mounted cowboy on a good-looking bay hackamore horse on the front cover. Will James put his 111 signature (see Signature Variations chapter) as a brand on the pony's left shoulder; I've never seen him use that as a brand before, or since. The jacket, like the book, has title and author in black ink on cover and

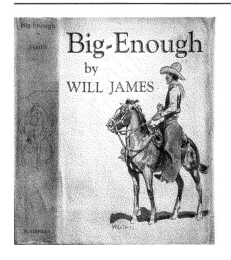

spine, with Scribners at the bottom of the spine. The middle third of the spine has a fine black line sketch of a pack horse on a light orange background. This book jacket spine, when in 'as new' condition, is the same beige as the front and rear and the orange background is clear and sharp. But when it gets sunned the beige turns browner and the orange fades; sometimes it fades out altogether. The rear of the jacket is a *Lone Cowboy* advertisement with a fine line drawing. The front foldover has a brief description of the book *Big Enough* and the rear foldover has quotes from three reviews of *Smoky*.

Pages: The pages start at Chapter 1 page 1 and go to page 314. The first edition has one free endpaper at the front of the book and one at the back.

Illustrations: There are 51 b&w drawings in *Big Enough* plus a photo frontispiece of Will James and his own little horse that he had named Big Enough.

Later Editions: After the first edition of *Big Enough* came out in October of 1931 with the 'A', Scribner's reprinted it again in 1931, with all details the same as in the first printing except without the 'A'. Only the two 1931 printings have the photo frontispiece.

In 1932 *Big Enough* was the fifth volume of the five-volume set produced in three states in 1932 and again in 1937 (see *Smoky* chapter for details).

Scribner's produced a 1939 reprint in a pale gray cover, same size as the first edition, same sketch on the front cover and same 314 pages. In 1944 they brought out the same book; 8-3/8" by 6", also with a light gray cover and 314 pages. The last Scribner's reprint that I have run across is a 1946 one the same as the 1944, except with a deep green cloth cover.

In the early 1950s World Publishing Company came out with a copy in green cloth; 8-1/4" by 5-3/4", still 314 pages.

Uncle Bill

A TALE OF TWO KIDS AND A COWBOY

1932

Contents: The book is in the form of an episodic short novel.

Comments: This first of the three *Uncle Bill* books is written on two levels. A children's book on the surface, but a primer for kids 7 to 77 who want to know what the real cowboy West was, and in some places still is, all about. In the modern sense it's a 'How To' book and makes easy, informative, and entertaining reading for any 'greenhorn' who wants to know about the <u>real thing</u>.

First Edition: The first edition of *Uncle Bill* was produced in 1932 in two states; both have the Scribner's 'A'. The book when first issued had a picture at the bottom of page 181 that illustrated the last line of the text above it: *"Only one spot showed in the dark of the night, that was Scootie's tent."* After only a few of that

first state
were issued,
some long-
gone and
unimaginative
art editor
must have
ordered a
change to a

galloping horse running to catch his bunch
and having nothing to do with the immediate
text. Maybe he couldn't read! The second
state of the first printing with the 'A', and all
subsequent reprints, have the horse picture.
The tent picture is never to be seen again!
That first state is very rare.

Size & Price: 8-1/2" high, by 6" deep, by 1-1/8" thick.
Price $2.00

Binding: Both first edition states are covered in orange
cloth with only black printing on cover and
spine. The cover has
the title at the top,
then subtitle, then
two line sketches of
the two youngsters
with lass ropes, plus
author at the bottom.
The spine has title,
subtitle, and author
at the top and
Scribners at the
bottom.

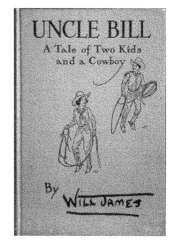

Dust Jacket: Beige paper with black illustrations on front and back covers and mostly black printing throughout. Front cover has title at the top and author at the bottom in red, black subtitle and illustration of the kids roping calves in the middle. (This illustration is also on page 217 of the book.) The spine has title in red at the top, then author, the sketch of Kip with a rope as on front cover of the book and on title page, and Scribners at the bottom, all in

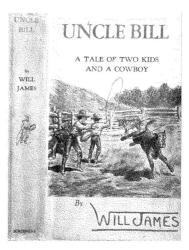

black ink. The rear of the dj has several nice little line sketches plus a fine drawing of a cowboy on horseback. It is mostly a pitch for four earlier Will James titles all at the price of $2.50 (probably all reprint editions). The front foldover is the Scribner's lead-in for the book, and the rear foldover has seven capsule reviews for seven of the eight previous Will James titles.

Pages: There are 241 numbered pages from 1 to 241. Both states of the first edition have one free endpaper at the front and one at the back of the book.

Illustrations: There are 61 separate b&w drawings in the book, plus the title page sketches are duplicated on the cover.

Later Editions: The first reprint, after the first two states of the first edition described above, also bears the 1932 date at the bottom of the title page. It is identical to the second state of the first edition in every way except the vital one: it does not have the Scribner's 'A'.

The same identical book was printed the next year with only the date changed to 1933 at the bottom of the title page. The next reprint in my records has 1936 at the bottom of the title page. The only other that I have seen is a 1946 wartime issue on thin paper. Same size and same 241 pages but only 1/2" thick. It is entirely possible that all these editions were printed from the same plates. The same typo on page 47 - 'to day' for 'today' - and at least one other, are carried right through to the 1946 edition.

None of the *Uncle Bill* books was licensed to other publishers.

LONE COWBOY

ILLUSTRATED CLASSIC EDITION

1932

Contents: As in my description of the first edition, this is a bio/novel or a fiction/ography.

Comments: The first and most important point to make is that, just the opposite from the *Smoky* Classic, the *Lone Cowboy* Classic is better than the first edition because it has 35 more examples of the wonderful Will James art than the original 1930 book, and yet includes, word for word and page for page, the entire text of the original. Another comment is that it is surely the most beautiful of all the Will James books that Scribner's ever produced, and they produced it for many decades.

First Issue: The first edition of *Lone Cowboy* came out in 1930 of course, but in 1932 Scribner's came out with this title in its large and lovely Illustrated Classic format. The printed text is identical to the first edition on every page from page 1 right through to page 431. It is my opinion that they printed both from the same plates.

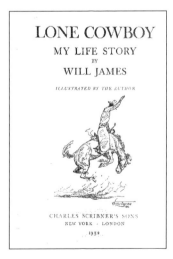

LONE COWBOY

MY LIFE STORY
BY
WILL JAMES

ILLUSTRATED BY THE AUTHOR

CHARLES SCRIBNER'S SONS
NEW YORK · LONDON
1932

The only way to tell if the *Lone Cowboy* Classic is a first state is by the date at the bottom of the title page. If it says 1932, it's a first printing. All subsequent copies in the original Classic format have later dates at the bottom of their title page, or no date.

Size & Price: 9-1/2" high, by 7-1/2" deep, by 1-1/2" thick. Original price: $1.75! Remember, 1932 was the depth of the Depression; buying books was an extravagance for many.

Binding: Scribner's produced many different books in the original Classic format through the 1930s and beyond.

Always the same height and depth and always in black cloth covers with a beautiful full-size full-color plate pasted onto the front cover and always with gold lettering on the spine. The *Lone Cowboy* Classic has title and "My Life Story" printed

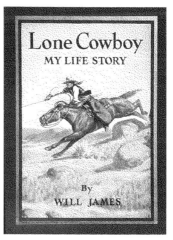

on the front cover color picture at the top, and has author at the bottom. The spine has title at the top, a very small sketch of a cabin under that, then author. At the middle of the spine it says "Illustrated by the Author" and at the bottom it says Scribners. All on spine is in gold ink.

69

Dust Jacket: The very first state and first issue of the *Lone Cowboy* Classic has a unique glassine dj and a blue/gray box with the book cover color picture pasted on the top. The dj is unique because it has front and back foldovers of pasted on and printed paper. The printing is lists of Scribner's Illustrated Classics books, 12 on the front foldover and 20 on the rear one. I believe that there were very few of the first printing in 1932 so produced. The majority of that 1932 issue were issued in a fine white paper dj with the same illustration and lettering on its front panel as that on the book. The spine has the same lettering and little cabin as on the book, but in black ink. The rear panel and the rear foldover are totally blank, and the front foldover nearly so. It has just four characters in the top right hand corner: $1.75. Most of the later years' djs have various printings on the rear panel and on one or both foldovers.

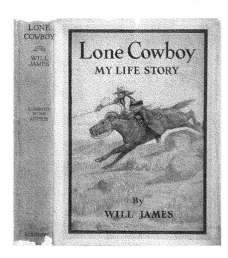

Pages: The text pages are numbered from 1 to 341. There are no free endpapers in these Illustrated Classics, just the colored two-page endpaper illustrations at the front and back.

Illustrations: There are 98 b&w drawings and eight full-color pictures in the Illustrated Classic edition of *Lone Cowboy*. These include all but two of the b&w drawings that are in the 1930 first edition, <u>plus 29 that are not in the first edition!</u> The eight colored plates are in addition to that, for a total of 106 pictures in all. The first edition had a Will James b&w portrait as a frontispiece that is not in the Classic, but it only had 71 total drawings. Of the eight colored plates, six are scattered throughout the text in unnumbered plates, one is the frontispiece, and one is in two places. The full double-page illustration is on the endpapers and paste-downs, front and back, in pale muted screen colors. The right-hand half of this painting, in much brighter and more vivid colors, is on the front cover of the book.

Later Editions: In the prewar years and through the 1940s, all the *Lone Cowboy* Scribner's Illustrated Classic books were the same size and format: black cloth covers, color picture pasted on the front cover, same picture as on inside covers and on djs and box covers; 9-1/2" by 7-1/4", 431 pages. Scribner's reproduced the *Lone Cowboy* Illustrated Classic in that format in 1936, '37, ('42 boxed), '45, '46, and '47 that I know of, and probably in other years. Sometime in about the 1950s, Scribner's converted their Illustrated Classic reprints to orange covers, but still with the same size and format; 9-1/2" by 7-1/4", 431 pages. The orange cover copies of *Lone Cowboy* that I've seen are undated at the bottom of the title page, and these orange or salmon colored copies usually had green djs with the same color illustration on the front as on all the others.

Scribner's never licensed other publishers to reprint their Illustrated Classics.

71

ALL IN THE DAY'S RIDING
1933

Contents: Full of 42 short stories and monographs, this fascinating book has more detail and more accurate cowboy lore than is in any other book anywhere. If you can't find answers to your cow and horse work questions here they probably don't exist!

Comments: Most, if not all of the 42 separate stories and monographs in the 12 chapters of this book previously appeared in *Sunset Magazine, Scribner's Magazine,* and others. Also a number are in other Will James books. It has already been touched upon above, but I'll repeat, this is certainly the most varied, most diversely illustrated, and most fully informative about the cowboy way of life of all the 24 Will James' books.

First Edition: There is one first-edition state with 1933 at the bottom of the title page and the 'A' right where it must always be, under the copyright data on the back side of the title page.

Size & Price: 9-1/2" high, by 7-3/8" deep, by 1-1/8" thick. Price $2.50

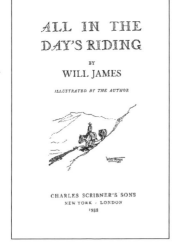

ALL IN THE
DAY'S RIDING

BY
WILL JAMES

ILLUSTRATED BY THE AUTHOR

CHARLES SCRIBNER'S SONS
NEW YORK · LONDON
1933

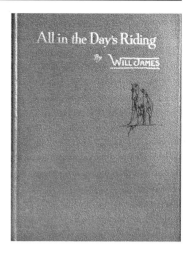

Binding: The first edition is in bright red cloth with a nice drawing of a cow pony saddled and 'ground hitched' (bridle reins to the ground) on the front cover in black ink. Title and author are at the top of the cover and spine, and Scribners is at the bottom of the spine, all in gold ink.

Dust Jacket: The dj is cream-colored paper. The front panel is a heavy red border around a black-on-white bucking horse picture. The cowboy is in the air, too far from the saddle to ever make it back! At the top of the jacket cover, the title is printed in black ink on the red background and the author is in the upper right-hand corner of the illustration. The title and author are at the top of the spine, a handsome horse's head adorns the middle, with the ever-present Scribners at the bottom, all in black ink on the cream paper. The horse's head drawing is also in the book at page 192. The back panel of the dj has the oft-repeated sketches of Will at

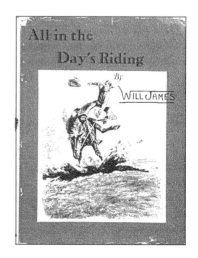

73

his drawing board with a montage of small figures and detail around and behind him. The back dj cover has a pitch for *Lone Cowboy,* and the front foldover is a blurb for this book, while the back one has some review quotes covering seven of Will James' previous titles.

Pages: The book starts at Chapter One page 1 and gallops through to 251. A single free endpaper is at the front of the book, but there are three of them at the back.

Illustrations: *All in the Day's Riding* has 104 separate b&w drawings in the book and 2 more on the dj that are not inside. This is by far the most for any of the 24 first-edition titles. If you want one of the best and most varied examples of Will James black-on-white art, which in my biased opinion is his genius medium, then perhaps one of the best single places to find it is in this book. Most of the 104 illustrations are signed and dated and they start with 1921 and go right up through 1932. That's 12 years of James' development and many examples of his finest work.

Chapter #1 — THE COWBOY TODAY, 4 stories, pages 1 - 14.

Chapter #2 — THE COWBOY'S
            WORK AND
            OUTFIT, 8 stories,
            pages 15 - 56.

Chapter #3 — THE CRITTER, 1 story, pages 57 - 63.

Chapter #4 — ALL IN THE DAY'S
            RIDING, 8 stories,
            pages 64 - 125.

Chapter #5 — ON THE DRIFT, 1 story,
            pages 127 - 135.

Chapter #6 — THE COWBOY
 CALENDER,
 12 stories, pages
 137-159.

Chapter #7 — THE RODEO,
 1 story,
 pages 160 - 180.

Chapter #8 — FOR A HORSE, 1 story, pages 181 - 192.

Chapter #9 — TOM & JERRY,
     3 stories,
     pages 193 - 213.

Chapter #10 — SCATTERED TRACKS, 1 story, pages 215 - 231.

Chapter #11 — FOLKS WEST,
     1 story,
     pages
     232 - 242.

Chapter #12 — HORSEFLESH, 1 story, pages 243 - 251.

Later Editions: Scribner's second printing in 1933 was identical to the first, except it had a 'B' in place of the 'A' on the copyright page. The next Scribner's printing, with 1936 on title page, was still the same in format, color, and size, but with more books listed opposite the title page and 'C' on the copyright page. The final and last Scribner's reprint was a wartime 1943 issue in a salmon-colored cloth cover. The same 9-1/2" high but only 6-5/8" deep, 251 pages and still an attractive Scribner's book.

World Publishing Company came out with a red cloth, 9-1/2" by 6-5/8" quite thin copy, stating on the copyright page "First Reprint Edition October 1945" and again in 1946 and 1948. Even though thinner than the Scribner's copies, it still had 251 pages, and all the wonderful drawings. Those are all the reprints that I have uncovered to date.

THE THREE MUSTANGEERS
1933

Contents: This book is a novel, and a most descriptive and entertaining one. It is about three cowboy partners who catch wild horses for a living and reduce the overstocking of the range at the same time. Mighty fine fellas but they tend to shade the law some here and there.

Comments: When I was a youngster in the 1930s and early '40s I used to run mustangs in even rougher country than Will describes in this book. We caught our share too, both roping them and trapping them. Some made fine cow horses too. It was exactly as Will James writes about it, and no one can bring it alive anywhere near as well as he can and does. This book is most particularly about people of the  West, and probably based around the turn of the century. There were plenty of pretty tough men in those times and this book gives a human touch to a few of them.

First Edition: This title came out in two states of the first edition. Both have 1933 at the bottom of the title page and the 'A' under the copyright. Both were printed and bound in the U.S.A. and in the U.K. and in exactly the same way except for the title page. The U.S. edition has New York - London under Charles Scribner's Sons at the bottom of the page. The U.K. edition has just London over Charles Scribner's Sons.

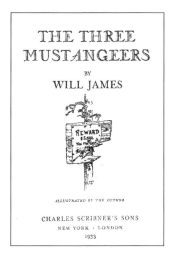

THE THREE
MUSTANGEERS

BY
WILL JAMES

ILLUSTRATED BY THE AUTHOR

CHARLES SCRIBNER'S SONS
NEW YORK · LONDON
1933

Size & Price: 8-1/2" high, by 6-1/8" deep, by 1-1/2" thick. Price: $2.75

Binding: Both first editions are covered in green cloth and have the title at the top of the front cover in gold, and author at the bottom in black ink. Also at the top right-hand corner they have a sketch of three horse's heads in black ink. The spine has the title and author at the top, and Scribners at the bottom all printed in gold.

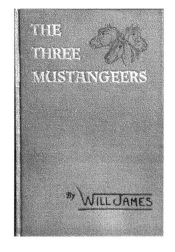

THE
THREE
MUSTANGEERS

By WILL JAMES

80

Dust Jacket: The same dj is used on both the U.S. and U.K. books, except for one minute detail: there is no price on the U.K. front foldover. The dj is white paper with all the written words — front, back, spine, and foldovers in blue ink. The front has the title at the top and author at the bottom. The front cover of the jacket has a delightful full-color picture of the three protagonists galloping down a wide trail with the lead man casually rolling a smoke on the run. The spine has title and author at the

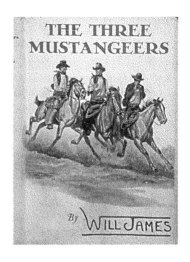

top and Scribners at the bottom. The rear cover has a picture of Will's face and ears shaded by a large cowboy hat screened in blue ink, plus offerings of 10 of his previous titles. The front foldover is the usual publisher's description of *The Three Mustangeers* and the rear foldover has two brief reviews of *All In The Day's Riding.*

Pages: The numbered pages start with page 3 at Chapter One and end at page 338. The two first editions have one free endpaper at the front of the book and one at the back.

Illustrations: There are 47 b&w sketches in this book including the dedication page sketch duplicated on the front cover. The b&w frontispiece is done in full color on the dust jacket.

81

Later Editions: Scribner's first reprint is the same as the first edition in covers, color, and size, but with 1934 at bottom of title page and no 'A'.

The last Scribner's reprint was dated 1944: green cloth cover with white lettering and the three horse's heads in white. Smaller in size, 8-1/4" by 6" and again a bit thinner, still 338 pages.

The World Publishing Co. brought out a Forum Books edition in a first printing in November of 1946. It also had the same 338 pages but was smaller still, 8-1/4" by 5-3/4" and only an inch thick. Forum made a second printing of this edition in January of 1947.

As good as this book is, it is surprising that it was not reprinted more often. At least it is great to know that The Mountain Press will be coming out with their fine reprint soon.

In the Saddle with Uncle Bill
1935

Contents: *In The Saddle* is in short novel form. It is the second novel in the *Uncle Bill* series.

Comments: Unlike the first, this second *Uncle Bill* is written primarily for young people. It carries on with the characters of the first book in the series, but is almost entirely a tale about one episode in the two kids' summer visit to their uncle's Five Barb ranch.

First Edition: The first edition of this book came out in only one state. It has 1935 at the bottom of the title page, and has the 'A' under the printing on the copyright page.

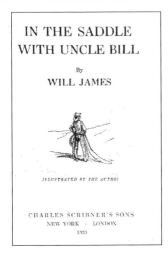

Size & price: 8-1/2" high, by 6" deep, by 1-3/8" thick. Price: $2.00

Binding: Green cloth binding with title at the top of the front cover and author near the bottom. There is a profile of a horse's head in a hackamore headstall just above the center of the front cover. The spine has the title at the top and Scribners at the bottom. The author is not mentioned on the spine and this is the only one of the Scribner's Will James first editions that has the title on the spine without the author. All the ink on spine and cover is black.

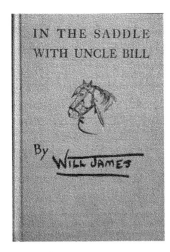

Dust Jacket: The dj on this book is a lovely bright red on most of the front cover and spine with all the printing in black ink. Title and author are on the cover and spine, but also the three principals are named and shown on the front cover.

Scribners is at the bottom of the spine as always. The bright red color on the spine is usually faded and often faded out completely. A fully red dj spine is very rare.

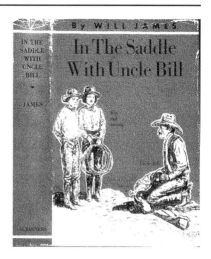

Pages: The book starts at Chapter One, page 3 and goes on to page 289. The final text page would be 290 but it is not numbered because there is a drawing at the bottom of the page in its place.

There is just one free endpaper at the front of the book and one at the back.

Illustrations: There are 38 b&w drawings in the book plus two on the dust jacket. The drawing on the front cover of the dj repeats the page 51 drawing in the book. That on the back of the dj is a repeat of the one on the back of the first *Uncle Bill -1932.* The front foldover is Scribner's review of the book, and the rear foldover has four fine and praising reviews of the first *Uncle Bill.*

Later Editions: Scribner's did not put out a Will James book in 1934, but published three in 1935; *In the Saddle, Young Cowboy,* and *Home Ranch.* Perhaps with that much production of one author in one year, fewer first editions of the two childrens' books were produced, making it hard to find firsts in any condition. Reprints are even more scarce. The only reprint of this title by Scribner's that I have seen is a wartime, 1944, very thin copy in pale green cloth — still with the same horse head in a hackamore on the cover; 8-3/8" by 6" and 290 pages.

None of the three *Uncle Bill* books was reprinted by other publishers.

Young Cowboy
1935

Contents: This is a children's book in novelette form for young boys and girls and was well received as such.

Comments: *Young Cowboy* has borrowings from many previous Will James books: *Smoky*, *Lone Cowboy*, *Sun Up*, and *Big Enough* among others. The final chapter is almost word for word from the last half of the 'Young Cowboy' chapter in *Sun Up*.

Dust jackets on well loved children's books often have a very low survival rate. The more loved the book the lower the rate. A first edition *Young Cowboy* <u>with dj</u> is rare and pricey indeed.

First Edition: The *Young Cowboy* first edition cover comes in two states; both have Scribner's first edition 'A' on the copyright page. The first state has a blue checked (gingham) cloth cover with a yellow label on the right-hand side of the front

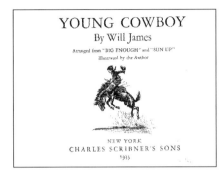

YOUNG COWBOY
By Will James
Arranged from "BIG ENOUGH" and "SUN UP"
Illustrated by the Author

NEW YORK
CHARLES SCRIBNER'S SONS
1935

cover. The label shows title, author, and a boy on a bucking pony printed in black ink. The second first edition cover is a solid pale blue cloth (no gingham checks), but is the same in all other details including the yellow label on the front cover and it also has the 'A'.

Size & Price: 7-1/4" high, by 9-7/8" deep, by 1/2" thick. Price: $1.50

Binding: As stated above, the first edition binding comes in two states. The first-state binding is with the blue checked (gingham) cloth cover and the second is the same in all details except it is covered in pale blue cloth. Both have the yellow label as described above, and neither has any writing on the spine.

Dust Jacket: The front of the jacket has a fine full-color, full-width picture of a young boy riding a bucking horse. The title is over the picture and the author under it, both in black ink. The spine of the dj is covered full length by the title and author, leaving no room for the usual 'Scribners' at the bottom of the spine. The back cover of the dj, printed in red, black, and blue, has a brief description of the story in the book plus a plug for three other Will

James books for boys and girls. The front foldover has a photo of, and brief note about, the author.

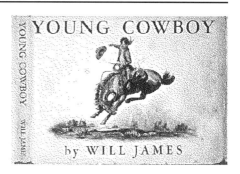

The rear foldover is blank.

Pages: This little book starts at Chapter One, page 1, and ends at page 72. The front and rear paste-downs are of yellow paper stock that continues to become the first free endpaper. Neither the front nor the back has a second free endpaper.

Illustrations: *Young Cowboy* has 31 b&w drawings and five full-color illustrations. In addition, the drawing on page 71 is at full size on the front cover label and at a reduced size on the title page. There is a nice hatted profile photo of James on the dj front foldover. The full-color frontispiece picture is reproduced at full size full color on the front of the dust jacket. It was done for the *Young Cowboy* book but the other four full-color pictures were done for the two Will James Illustrated Classics, *Smoky* and *Lone Cowboy,* two pictures from each. Many of the b&w pictures came from previous books as well.

Later Editions: This was a good and very popular Will James book. The first Scribner's reprint was 1936; same size with 72 pages, but cover is light brown cloth and there is no yellow label. The name, author, and same cover picture are printed in black directly on the cloth on the left side of the front cover. The next two reprints that I've seen are 1938 and 1940 and are almost identical to the first edition, second state — pale blue cloth, printed yellow label, same size and same 72 pages. A 1945 Scribner's reprint was about the same as the 1936 first reprint, but with the picture, name, and author printed on the right side of the light tan cloth cover. Undated copies with Scribner's code on copyright page suggesting 1962 and 1965 reprint editions are the same as the 1945 edition above. It is likely that Scribner's reissued it more times than those noted above. No other publisher was licensed to print Young *Cowboy*.

A Collection of Will James Books

olors of the binding and dust jackets are important for collectors.
ome first editions, including some with the Scribner 'A', have
een rebound. These may be either library of former owner
binds.

he following pages show color reproductions of all the first
lition bindings and the first state dust jackets (djs). All of the
ctures were taken from books and djs in the author's personal
ollection that has been assembled and upgraded over several
ecades. Some of the djs have small flaws, but are proven first
ate. Sun fading causes colors to vary somewhat from those
own here.

or reading and owning Will James' wonderful books, stories,
id pictures, Scribner's copies are best. First edition, first state
pies in fine condition can be very pricey and are usually of
remost importance only to true collectors.

Lone Cowboy
Limited Edition
1930

Scribner's published 250 copies of this limited edition. Details of this book are pretty well described in the *Lone Cowboy* chapter, pages 40-47. However, the colors of the slipcase need a few addtional words.

The relatively fragile paper slipcase, covered in a pale green paper oddly sensitive to light and sun, was originally about the same color as the book cover. If it had been kept in a darkened room for most of its nearly seven decades, it would still be green, but even in open book shelves in a windowed room, the spine and top of the case darkens and soon turns brown on the exposed surfaces.

The copy shown here has the spine color just about as dark as the leather spine label. I've had lighter copies, but none that were as pale on the spine as the green on the sides of the slipcase.

slip
case
spine

book
spine

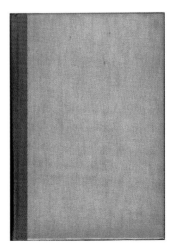

book cover

1924

Cowboys
North
and
South

page 1

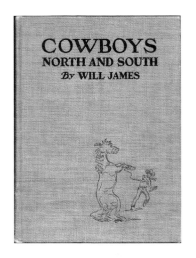
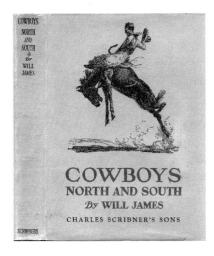

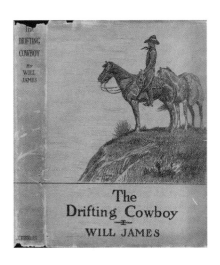

1925

The
Drifting
Cowboy

page 9

1926

Smoky

page 16

ate C

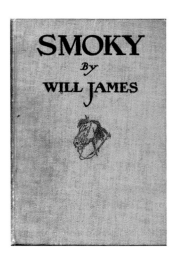
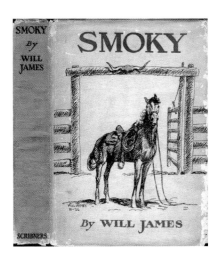

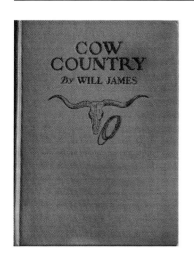

1927

Cow
Country

page 22

1929

Sand

page 31

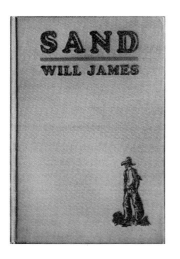

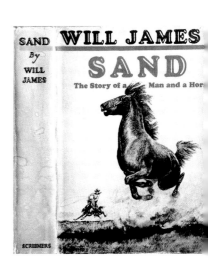

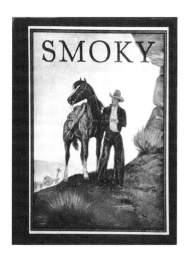

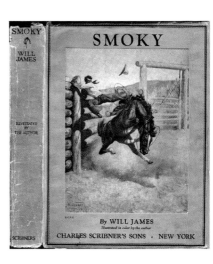

1929

Smoky
(classic)

page 35

plate

1930

Lone
Cowboy

page 40

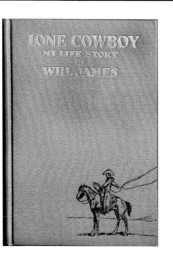

1931

Sun Up

page 48

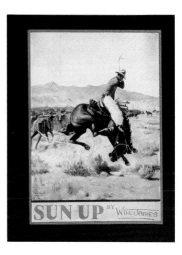

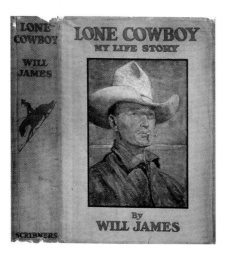

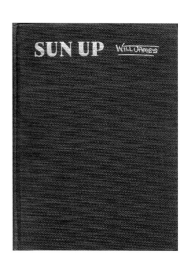

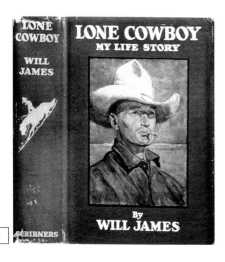

ate E

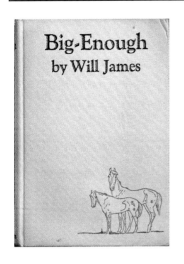

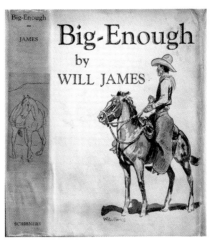

1931

Big Enough

page 60

1932

Uncle Bill

page 64

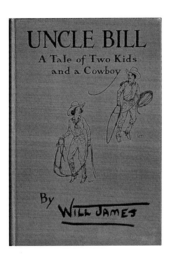

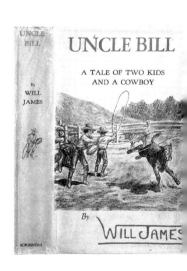

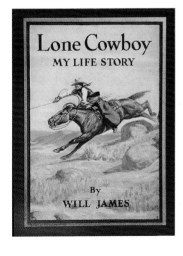

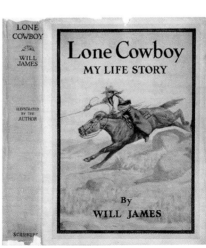

1932

Lone Cowboy
(Classic)

page 68

plate

1933

All In The
Days Riding

page 72

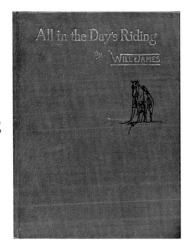
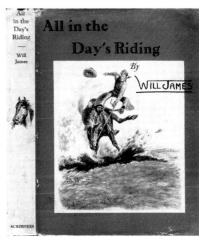

1933

The Three
Mustangers

page 79

1935

In The Saddle
with Uncle
Bill

page 83

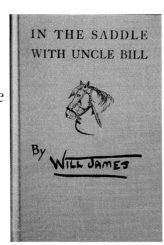
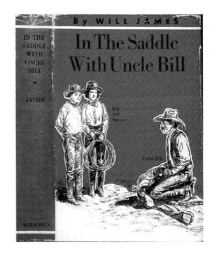

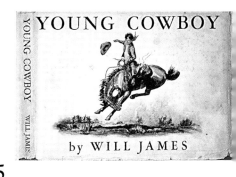

1935

Young Cowboy   page 87

1935

Home
Ranch

page 91

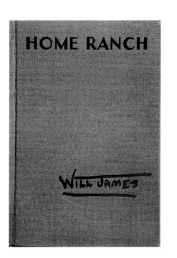
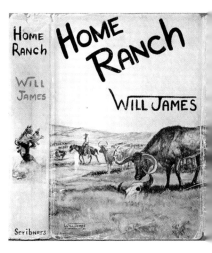

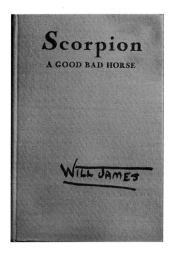
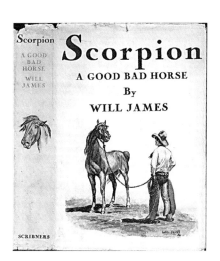

1936

Scorpion

page 100

plate F

1937

Cowboy
In The
Making

page 104

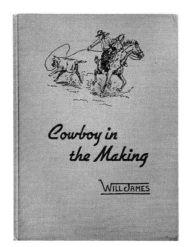

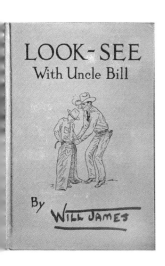
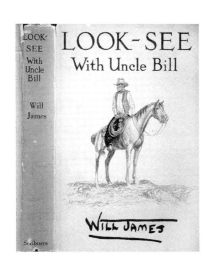

1938

Look See
with
Uncle Bill

page 112

1938

Will James
Cowboy
Book

page 115

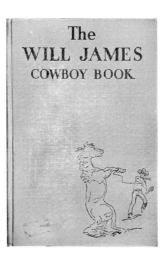

plate I

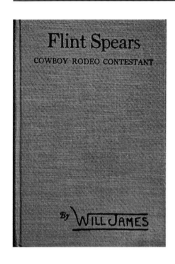

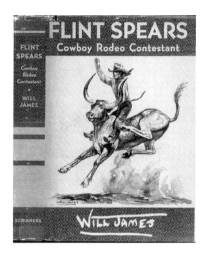

1938

Flint Spears

page 120

1939

The
Dark Horse

page 130

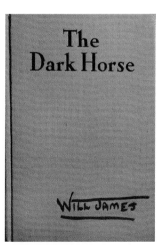

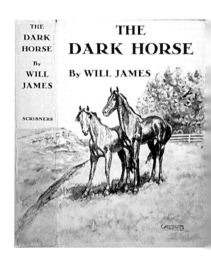

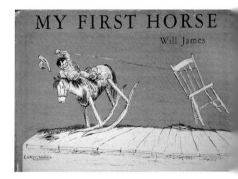

1940

My First Horse   page 134

1940

Horses
I've
Known

page 137

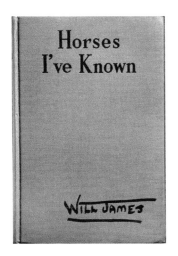

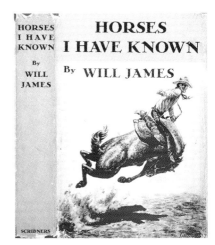

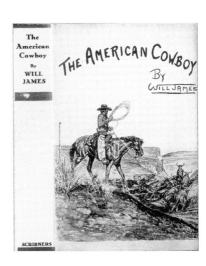

1942

The
American
Cowboy

page 145

1951

Will James
Book of
Cowboy
Stories

page 155

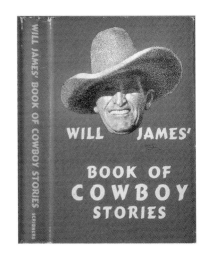

HOME RANCH
1935

Contents: Although in the general form of a Will James novel, I include this with his books of short stories. While the primary characters and location are carried through the book, the chapters are self-contained and are titled as short episodes. Try Chapter 9 if you like to laugh.

Comments: In spite of the weakness of some of the illustrations, as stated below, this is a good and descriptive book about cowboying and ranch work. The presence of the obnoxious dudes in the story gives clear examples of, and graphic counterpoint to, the many and varied skills that a real cowboy must have to get every day's work done. You don't learn those skills in just weeks and months. Some don't learn them in years and years.

First Edition: Home Ranch was printed twice in 1935 but only the first printing has the 'A'. Both printings have 1935 at the bottom of the title page.

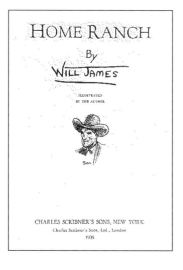

Size & Price: 8-1/2" high, by 6" deep, by 1-1/2" thick. Price: $2.75

Binding: The book is bound in warm brown cloth with black ink lettering on the cover and spine. Front cover has title at the top and author near the bottom. Spine has title and author at the top with Scribners at the bottom.

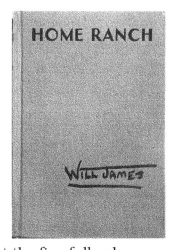

Dust Jacket: The dj is unique in that the fine full-color picture on the front cover is printed 7-1/2" wide and wraps 1-1/2" onto the foldover! This unusual detail occurs on the subsequent

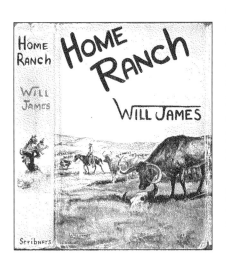

Scribner's reprints also. The dj has title and author on the front cover and title, Scribners, and an illustration on the spine, all in black ink. The author is on the spine under the title in red ink. The spine illustration first appeared in *Smoky* in 1926. The back panel of the dj has the big hatted 'head & ears' photo of James that was first printed on *The Three Mustangeers* dj.

Pages: Starting at Chapter One, page 3, the book ends at page 346. There is one free endpaper at the front of the book and two at the back.

Illustrations: There are 54 b&w drawings in this book plus a full-color painting, a drawing, and a screened photo on the dust wrapper.

In *'The Spirit of the Cowboy'* Abe Hays states: "The down side of Will James' art was reached in the pencil drawings in *Home Ranch.* The vast majority of its drawings are simply crude and inept by any standard. His drinking was the problem."

Chapter #1 — RIDING BOG
 Pages 3 to 23, with three drawings.

Two young cowboys doing tough and miserable work in the month of March. Then two old ones reminiscing about their times in bygone decades.

Chapter #2 — FIRST HERDS AND NEW RANGES
 Pages 24 to 36, with two drawings.

Reminiscences by the old cowman who started the 7 Xs Ranch, which is the outfit where all these stories occur.

93

Chapter #3 — COWBOYS OLD AND NEW
      Pages 37 to 52, with two drawings.

The 'Old Man' John B. starts to turn the ranch over to his son Austin, with mixed feelings for sure.

Chapter #4 — HARD WINTERS AND DRY SUMMERS
      Pages 53 to 75, with three drawings.

Son Austin goes away to World War I and daughter June grows up. Life goes on at the 7 Xs. The depression of the 1930s comes along too, but the ranch holds its own.

Chapter #5   SPRING AND ROUND-UPS
      Pages 76 to 103, with four drawings.

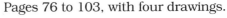

Descriptions of the round-up wagons and starting out for the round-up. Telling of the preparations, including gathering of the horse herd to select 4- and 5-year-olds to break in for remuda replacements. A very fine and descriptive short story chapter.

Chapter #6 — LONGHORNS FOR KEEPS
Pages 104 to 130, with three drawings.

This chapter covers an old cowman's philosophy for happiness - particulary on page 106, though it goes further on the subject as it goes along. The last part of the chapter is a skit about two old mossy-backed longhorn steers that have escaped the upgrading of the herd.

Chapter #7 — STRANGERS TO CAMP
Pages 131 to 142, with two drawings.

This marks the invasion of a band of dudes who play havoc with the working round-up for the next few chapters.

95

The dudes
settle in for an
uninvited stay
— unfortu-
nately.

A hilarious
tale about
the dudes
causing
not one
chuck
wagon
runaway,
but two!

A classic thunder and
lightning cloudburst
catching the dudes
entirely unprepared.
There's hope that a
soaking will send them
away. It doesn't.

Chapter #11 — HELL AND HIGH WATER
Pages 223 to 239, with three drawings.

The dudes get
flooded out,
but their car
gets flooded
in. That car is
not going to
leave the
bottom of
that wash
under its own
power no-how!

Chapter #12 — "WHEN THE COWS COME HOME"
Pages 240 to 260, with three drawings.

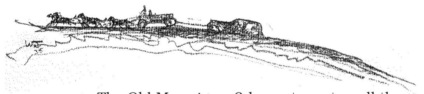

The Old Man rigs a 6-horse team to pull the car and dudes to the ranch.

Chapter #13 — "A DIFFERENT KIND OF THE SAME BREED"
Pages 261 to 279, with three drawings.

A single college-boy
dude, friend of
daughter June,
comes out to the
ranch. The boy,
Dale, is less of a
parasite, fortunately,
but a pure green-
horn nevertheless.

Chapter #14 — "ONE UP AND THREE TO GO" Pages 280 to 303, with four drawings.

Dale has a few amusing adventures but is most useful in figuring out a way to get the three parasites away for good.

Chapter #15 — "REGULAR RANCH VS. DUDE RANCH" Pages 304 to 324, with three drawings.

Will James describes different kinds of dude ranches, including real ranches that run dudes as a sideline. He also describes dude 'resorts' that are entirely dude operations and 'ranches' in name only.

Chapter #16 — HOME RANCH
Pages 325 to 346, with two drawings.

This final chapter sort of ties the whole book together. June gets the cowboy she has always wanted and long had an 'under-standing' with. Son 'Austin' is running the ranch well and profitably. 'The Old Man' gathers the loose ends of his ranching philosophy into a final and fine package. Life and ranching are good.

Later Editions: Scribner's did a second printing in 1935, the same in every detail except no 'A' under the copyright. And they did a third printing, the same again, but with the date 1936 at the bottom of the title page and no 'A'.

World Publishing Co. reprinted *Home Ranch* at least four times, all 8-5/8" by 5-7/8" by 1", 346 pages.

1. 'First Forum Edition' August 1945, brown cover.

2. Second printing October 1945, same brown cover.

3. 'World Reprint Edition' first printing, October 1948, salmon/tan cover.

4. World Publishing Co., second printing, October 1951.

In 1946 Bantam Books produced a paperback edition for 25 cents (!); 6-3/8 by 4-1/8", with all 16 stories and all but two or three of the drawings. All condensed into 279 pages and with a colored cover by an inferior artist.

SCORPION

A GOOD BAD HORSE

1936

Contents: This is another Will James novel with a horse as a central character. And this horse is one rough hombre. His rider isn't plumb gentle either but the horse wins the decisive battles and makes everything come out right in the end.

Comments: This is again a story where Will carries on with his oft-held position that some of the cowboys who skate on thin ice with the law are really good guys and those good guys always turn out well at the end. Since his own life and past included brushes with the law, he spent a certain amount of his writing time trying to justify and dress up his — and some of his friends' — past actions. But that aside, this is a dandy story, well told and nicely illustrated, a fun read. As always with Will James books, full of cow, cowboy, and horse lore. This one has a nice cowgirl too.

First Edition: The first edition of *Scorpion* comes in only one state. It has the 1936 date at the bottom of the title page and the 'A' on the copyright page.

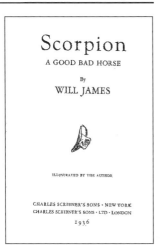

Scorpion

A GOOD BAD HORSE

By

WILL JAMES

ILLUSTRATED BY THE AUTHOR

CHARLES SCRIBNER'S SONS · NEW YORK
CHARLES SCRIBNER'S SONS · LTD · LONDON

1936

Size & Price: 8-1/2" high, by 6-1/8" deep, by 1-1/2" thick. Price: $2.50

Binding: Scribner's bound this in a tasteful rust-brown cloth with black printing on the cover and spine. The cover and spine have the title at the top with the subtitle directly underneath. The cover has the author near the bottom, but the spine has the author directly under the subtitle. The spine has Scribners at the bottom.

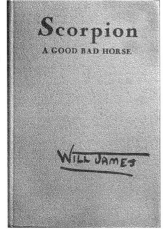

Dust Jacket: To find a first edition of this book in a very fine dust jacket is next door to impossible. There are plenty of first-edition copies around and a fair number in djs ... but ... try finding a dj with the red-ink lettering on the spine! The red ink fades to pink very easily and soon after that disappears altogether. This book has a very pretty dust jacket with a full-color picture on the front cover showing a cowboy standing gazing at a fine-looking horse. Over the picture in blue ink are the title, subtitle, and author. The spine has the title at the top and Scribners at the bottom in blue ink. Under the title are the subtitle and author, originally in deep red ink, and at the middle of the spine a full-color horse head, and that pony is in a bad mood. The rear panel has the screened hatted bust of James plus a list of Scribner's previously published Will James books all in blue ink, and the author in red ink at the top of the hat. The front foldover has the publisher's description of the book, and the rear one

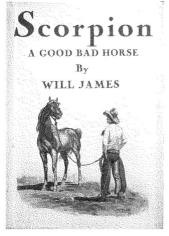

a list of three earlier Will James 'Young Readers' titles with a New York newspaper review of each. If your copy of the dj has the red ink on the spine, it is easy to tell how much it may have faded by opening the foldover and comparing the red ink on that with what's on your spine. When issued they were the same color.

Pages: *Scorpion* starts at Chapter One, page 5 and ends at page 312. There is one free endpaper at the front of the book and one at the rear.

Illustrations: This book has one full-color frontispiece plus 45 b&w drawings and some good ones too. The front of the dj has the frontispiece full-color illustration, the spine has the horse's head in color; the screened and hatted bust of James in blue ink is on the back.

Later Editions: Scribner's never reprinted this title as far as I know. Grosset & Dunlap reprinted it at least twice: once in 1939 and again in 1949. (The two different states of dust jackets have codes of 39 and 49 respectively.)

There are no other known reprints.

COWBOY IN THE MAKING
1937

Contents: *Cowboy in the Making* was put together as a children's book and it is entirely a work of fiction. Each chapter is a titled freestanding story, though they are strung together as a narrative, so for people who like Will James' short stories I've treated them as such.

Comments: These little chapters are nice bedtime stories for parents who like to read to their young children. Since the eleven stories in this book were entirely assembled from the first seven chapters of *Lone Cowboy* there is really nothing new here, but it is better organized for short story reading to or by youngsters.

First Edition: The first edition of this book came out in only one state and that is clearly recognizable, with 1937 at the bottom of the title page and the Scribner's 'A' on the copyright page.

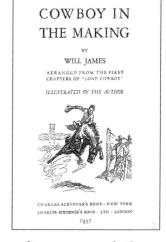

COWBOY IN
THE MAKING
BY
WILL JAMES
ARRANGED FROM THE FIRST
CHAPTERS OF "LONE COWBOY"
ILLUSTRATED BY THE AUTHOR

CHARLES SCRIBNER'S SONS · NEW YORK
CHARLES SCRIBNER'S SONS · LTD · LONDON
1937

Size & Price: 9-1/2" high, by 7-1/4" deep, by 3/4" thick. Price: $1.50

Binding: The book is bound in a medium green cloth with the print and lettering all in dark blue ink. The front cover has a picture of a boy roping a calf from on horseback at the top, title in the middle, and author under that.

The title and author are printed along the spine with Scribners in very small print at the bottom.

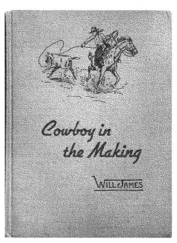

Dust Jacket: An almost suspicious number of first-edition copies of this book are to be found in fine-condition dust jackets. Suspicious because it is most unusual for the djs to survive well if the book has been actually read or handled by children. The jacket is white paper with the same full-color illustration as the frontispiece, which is also the same calf-roping picture that appears as a line drawing on the book's binding cover. Under the picture in black ink are the title and author. Along the spine are also title and author plus Scribners at the bottom, all in black ink. The rear panel of the dj has a very nice photo of Will at his drawing board in his log cabin studio. The photo is bordered in hot pink! The front foldover describes the book as usual, but the rear one advertises a Scribner's book not by Will James. This is unusual.

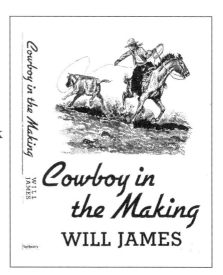

Pages: The book starts at Chapter One, page 1 and ends at page 91. There is one free endpaper at the front of the book and one at the rear.

Illustrations: Most of the drawings in this book come from *Lone Cowboy,* just as all of the text was extrapolated from there. The frontispiece in color was first done for this book and is also used in full color on the front of the dj. In addition, a line rendition of the same picture is on the front cover of the book. There are 25 b&w drawings in the book. Also, there are three full-color illustrations scattered in the text, two from the *Lone Cowboy* Illustrated Classic, and one first used on the cover of *Sun Up.*

Chapter #1 — A COWBOY COMES TO MONTANA
Pages 1 - 6 with two drawings. Early beginnings of Billy's dad and mother coming to Montana.

Chapter #2 — FIRST RIDING
Pages 7 - 17 with two full-

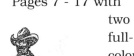

color illustrations and two drawings. Billy gets his first horse and first saddle and takes to both like a duck to water. The 'old timer' is introduced and Billy calls him Bopy. At the end of the chapter Billy is 'left' to old trapper Jean - 'Bopy.'

Chapter #3 — THE OLD TIMER TAKES ME ALONG
Pages 18 - 27 with two drawings.
Billy does some
early growing,
living out with
Bopy, and after
nearly a year
finds out that his
dad is dead.
Billy takes that
news pretty hard
but learns to
look for what's
"over the next
mountain."

Chapter #4 — PAPER AND PENCIL
Pages 28 - 32 with two drawings.
Bopy gives Billy his first pad of paper and
pencils and the youngster starts right away to
draw with them.

Chapter #5 — WINTER CAMP
Pages 33 - 40 with two drawings.

Young Billy starts his education with the pictures in old magazines and then, as a young fellow might, he drank some lye by misadventure and laid himself up in camp for most of the winter. Bopy also started Billy to reading from the catalogs and taught him numbers too.

Chapter #6 — COWBOYS AGAIN
Pages 41 - 47 with one full-color illustration and two drawings.

The following summer it was back to cowboying again, and they spent the next winter trapping at one of the ranch cow camps.

Chapter #7 — THE COW CAMP
        Pages 48 - 56 with
        two drawings.
        Billy gets lots of
        practice that
        winter, riding,
        roping, reading,
        and drawing. He
        gets given a new
        horse.

Chapter #8 — DRIFTING NORTH
        Pages 57 - 66 with
        one drawing.
        Bopy heads up into Canada and Billy sees his
        first town, actually stays in a hotel too. Also,
        Billy discovers that there are other kids in the
        world; he'd only seen grown-ups before. They
        leave their horses there, much to Billy's re-
        gret, and then go much further north to an
        old camp of Bopy's where they spend a long
        winter.

Chapter #9 — MY FIRST RIFLE
Pages 67 - 74 with
two drawings.
Billy is up to
about 9 or 10
years old by
now and Bopy
gives him a big
old muzzle-
loading gun
and teaches
him how to use
it. The young-
ster has a lot of
good experiences with that gun as a companion, and helps get ducks and rabbits for
dinner too.

Chapter #10 — A BEAR ON THE ROOF
Pages 75 - 80 with two drawings.
Once while Bopy was away overnight on his
trapping rounds, a bear came around the
cabin. Old Bruin smelled the meat cache in
the lean-to at the
back and went to
breaking in. Billy
took his gun out
and with a lucky
shot killed the
bear. Bopy was
amazed and
pleased when he
returned, but
mighty glad that
Billy hadn't gotten
the worst of it.

Chapter #11 — GROS AND OTAY

Pages 81 - 91 with three drawings.

In this final chapter Billy is a year older and he and Bopy winter in at Bopy's main camp up in Canada. It has more supplies for Billy's reading and drawing, and Billy has two pets to keep him company. The pets are a pair of young orphan wolves! The wolves, named Gros and Otay, are good friends for Billy that winter but they run off with a passing wild wolf pack in the spring. That summer Billy is reunited with his beloved horses, and this book ends.

Later Editions: Scribner's did at least three reprints with 91 pages and the same format.

1939 Light green cloth covers; 9-3/8" by 7-1/4"

1949 Gray cloth covers; 9-1/8" by 7-1/4"

1969 (?) Reddish brown cloth covers; 9-3/8" by 7-1/8"

Scribner's never gave out rights to other publishers to reprint the six Will James books written specifically for children; hence there are no non-Scribner's reprints of this book.

LOOK-SEE

WITH UNCLE BILL

1938

Contents: *Look-See* is in narrative form and details Kip & Scootie's third summer out on their uncle's ranch. Again episodic, it starts with a cattle drive, intersperses an adventure in an abandoned mine shaft, and then a flood. After the

drive, and back at the home ranch, the two kids set out to rebuild the tumbled-down first cabin built at the ranch by their grandfather. The book ends with a lion hunt at the old mine shaft that the kids had found on the cattle drive.

Comments: It seems to me that there were fewer copies of this book produced than of the other two *Uncle Bill* books, and that applies to the reprints as well as to the first edition. In any case it certainly is more scarce in the marketplace. The wonderful 'Old Timer,' Uncle Bill, is present in this story too but has a lesser role than in the first two.

First Edition: This is the third and last book of the *Uncle Bill* series; it has only one first-edition state. It has 1938 at the bottom of the title page and was not reprinted in 1938. The Scribner's 'A' is in its usual position under the copyright.

LOOK-SEE
With Uncle Bill
BY WILL JAMES

ILLUSTRATED BY THE AUTHOR

NEW YORK
CHARLES SCRIBNER'S SONS
1938

Size & Price: 8-1/2" high, by 6" deep, by 1-1/8" thick. Price $ 2.00

Binding: The book is bound in a strong blue cloth, and all the writing and the sketch are in black ink. The front cover has the title at the top with the subtitle under it and the author at the bottom. The middle of the cover has a line sketch of Uncle Frank helping young Kip fit into a new pair of chaps. The sketch appears as a more finished drawing on page 21 of the book. The spine has the title, subtitle, and author, in order down from the top, and Scribners at the bottom.

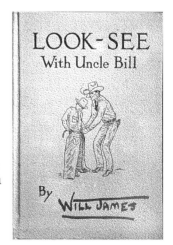

Dust Jacket: The cream-colored dj has a full-color reproduction of the full-color frontispiece illustration in the middle of the front panel, the title and subtitle over it and the author under it.

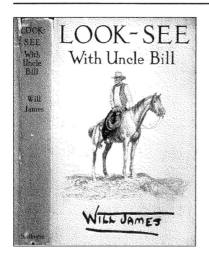

The spine, like the binding, has title, subtitle and author at the top with Scribners at the bottom. The rear panel promotes the first two *Uncle Bill* books and has a nice old drawing from page 45 of *Smoky* (1926) at the bottom. The front foldover is the book description as always and the rear one lists seven Will James books. All the wording on the dj is in black ink.

Pages: *Look-See* starts on page 3 and ends at (unnumbered) page 254. The last page has a drawing at the end in place of a last page number. There is one free endpaper at the front of the book and one at the rear.

Illustrations: This book has one full-color frontispiece and 36 b&w drawings. The drawing on page 21 is repeated in line form on the front cover of the book. The jacket has a repeat of the frontispiece, in color, and one b&w drawing repeated from *Smoky*.

Later Editions: Scribner's reprinted this title at least twice more in a similar size and format, and the reprints also end at page 254. The first reprint that I have seen is dated 1945 and is in darker gray-green cloth covers, 8-1/2" by 6". The only other Scribner's reprint that I've come across was dated 1951. It had light gray cloth covers, and was 8-1/2" by 6-1/8".

There may well be other Scribner's reprints, but there are no reprints of any of the *Uncle Bill* books by other publishers.

THE WILL JAMES COWBOY BOOK
1938

Contents: This is a book of previously published Will James short stories and excerpted stories from his novels. They are geared toward his younger fans because the book (according to Jeff Dykes, a respected authority) was intended to be offered as a supplementary reader to the Texas (and perhaps other states') State Department of Education. It missed that market and presumably only a very small number of copies was distributed. There are surely very few around and it is probably the most rare Will James book.

Comments: This book was entirely assembled by Scribner's editor Alice Dalgliesh from stories and pictures published in seven previous books by Will James. Scribner's was finding it most difficult to get Will to meet production schedules and deadlines in these, his heavy drinking years. That contributed to his having little or nothing to do with the material in this book. Also, from 1938 on, Scribner's removed most dates from under Will's signature on pictures they reused from earlier books. They probably did not want the readers to realize they were seeing older pictures in newer books.

First Edition: The first edition of this book is the only edition of this book and it is very scarce indeed. There is no date on the title page, but the copyright page has the 1938 date and the Scribner's 'A'.

Size & Price: 8-1/4" high, by 5-7/8" deep, by 3/4" thick. There is no record that this book was ever offered for general retail sale, and it is most unlikely that it was ever so offered. Price - if any - is unknown.

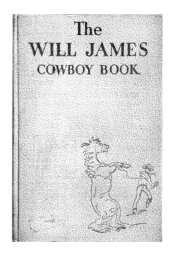

THE WILL JAMES
COWBOY BOOK

BY

WILL JAMES

Edited by
ALICE DALGLIESH

CHARLES SCRIBNER'S SONS · NEW YORK
Chicago · Boston · San Francisco · Atlanta · Dallas

Binding: The book was bound in orange cloth with all printing and sketch in black ink on cover and spine. The front cover has the full title at the top and a re-production of a line drawing of a cowboy front-footing a horse in the bottom right-hand corner. The drawing is the same one that is on the cover of *Cowboys North and South,* Will's first book (1924). The spine has the title at the top with a line under the last word and Scribners at the bottom.

Dust Jacket: No dj has ever been seen with this book and it was almost certainly issued in its very limited numbers without one.

Pages: The book starts at page 5 and the text ends at page 158. Following page 158 there are two unnumbered pages. The first is a page full of brands explaining those shown at page 82 of the book. And the second is a list of the seven earlier Will James books from which this book's stories were excerpted.

Illustrations: The one colored frontispiece and all the b&w illustrations have appeared in previously published Will James books. Also the black-on-orange rear paste-down drawing first appeared on the dust wrapper of *Lone Cowboy* 1930, and was repeated on others. The other four black-on-orange drawings on the front and back endpapers all come from illustrated letters Will sent to his publishers. This is stated in the last paragraph on the rear end paper. (I'm fortunate enough to own one of the letters that has three of these drawings, plus a few more they didn't use here.) All told there are one full-color frontispiece and 48 b&w drawings in the book, five black-on-orange ones on the end papers and one on the front cover.

The list of stories follows by title and previously published book source(s).

A YOUNG COWBOY

Story #1 — Billy Goes to the Round-Up - *Young Cowboy,* Chapter 7

Story #2 — Billy Breaks His First Bronc - *Young Cowboy,* Chapter 12

Story #3 — A Bear on the Roof - *Lone Cowboy*, Chapter 6
& *The Making of a Cowboy*, Chapter 10

Story #4 — The Pet Wolves - *Lone Cowboy*, Chapter 7
& *The Making of a Cowboy*, Chapter 11

Story #5 — A COWBOY'S YEAR - *All In The Day's Riding*,
Chapter 6

January - Bucking the Snowdrifts

February - The End of a Killer

March- The First Blades of Grass

April - Gathering the Saddle
Horses

May - The Spring Round-Up

June- The Horse Round-Up

July - Riding for a Prize

August - Breaking Broncs

September - Line Riders

October - Cutting Out

November - The End of the
Season

December- The Winter Camp

ON THE RANCH WITH UNCLE BILL

Story #6 — About Cowboys - mostly from *All in the Day's
Riding*, Chapter 2

Story #7 — About Roping -
edited from
Uncle Bill,
Chapter 1

Story #8 — About Branding -
edited from
Uncle Bill,
Chapter 10

Story #9 — Kip and Scootie Have an Adventure - from *Look See*, Chapter 6

Story #10 — Uncle Bill Tells a Story - from *Uncle Bill*, Chapter 7

HORSES AND THEIR WAYS

Story #11 — Smoky, the Range Colt - from *Smoky*, Chapter 1

Story #12 — Tom and Jerry - from *All in the Day's Riding*, Chapter 9

SOME COWBOY ADVENTURES

Story #13 — A Tight Squeeze - first book appearance was in *All in the Day's Riding*, then titled "Up in the Eagle Territory"

Story #14 — A Narrow Escape - first book appearance was in *All in the Day's Riding*, then titled "Down the Wash"

Later Editions: There were no later editions of this title, none by Scribner's and none by anyone else either.

FLINT SPEARS

COWBOY RODEO CONTESTANT

1938

Contents: This is again a Will James book of short stories with one central character carrying through from start to finish.

Comments: Will James knew rodeoing from all sides. He contested in them, put on a few with his friends, wrote news commentaries on them, and acted as a judge in quite a few. These stories give plenty of examples of how rough a game rodeoing is. Unlike participants in most professional sports, the rodeo cowboy gets no salary or benefits. He even has to put up entry fees to get into the contest, and gets prize money only if he wins any. He pays his own travel and room and board and his own inevitable hospital bills when he gets hurt.

First Edition: *Flint Spears* came out in two first-edition states; neither has the Scribner's 'A'. Both have 1938 at the bottom of the title page and both have the 18 pages of 21 rodeo photographs at the back of the book. The first state is the U.S. edition with 'New York' over Scribner's name at the bottom of the title

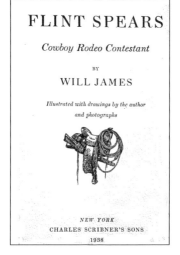

FLINT SPEARS

Cowboy Rodeo Contestant

BY

WILL JAMES

*Illustrated with drawings by the author
and photographs*

NEW YORK
CHARLES SCRIBNER'S SONS
1938

120

page, and the book is bound in orange cloth. The second first edition state is the U.K. edition bound in a pale blue cloth and with 'London' over Scribner's name at the bottom of the title page. In all other details the two are the same. This title is the only Will James book after the first five where the first editions do not have the Scribner's 'A'. When asked about it, Scribner's claimed it to have been an oversight. As will be stated in 'Later Editions' below, the second printing in 1938 says "Second Printing, November 1938" on the copyright page. This was not the normal Scribner's practice.

Size & Price: 8-1/2" high, by 6" deep, by 1-1/4" thick. Price: U.S. $2.50; U.K. price is unknown.

Binding: The U.S. edition is bound in orange cloth with very dark blue-black ink printing on the cover and spine. The front cover has the title at the top with subtitle underneath it and author at the bottom. On the spine, title is at the top, author in the middle, and Scribners at the bottom. Each is bracketed over and under by heavy 5/16" bands of ink going all across the spine, total six bands. The U.K. edition is bound in pale blue cloth with black ink printing on the cover and spine. The front cover has title at the top, no subtitle, and author just under the title. The

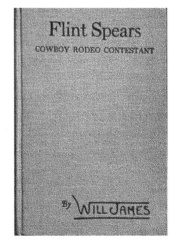

spine has title and author at the top with a short heavy line between them, and Scribners at the bottom. The six heavy bands are not present.

Dust Jacket: The off-white paper djs on the two first-edition states are the same on covers and spine but differ on the foldovers. The middle of the front cover has a grand full-color picture of a cowboy riding a longhorn steer, the same picture as the frontispiece in the book.

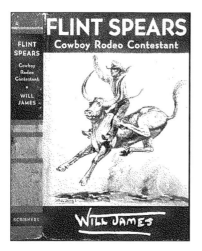

The title and subtitle are over, and the author under, the picture; both are on a gray background. The spine has seven red bands variably placed. The printing is on the same gray background as the cover with title, subtitle, and author at the top and Scribners at the bottom. The rear cover has the photograph of a bucking horse and rider that is also the first one of the rodeo photos shown at the back of the book. Below the photo is a continuation of the Scribner's text about the book's contents. There is no red ink used on the back cover of the dj. The front and rear foldovers have text in both red and black ink. The front one has the price, $2.50, at the top on the U.S. edition, but there is no price at the top on the U.K. edition. Again, the front foldover describes the book, and the rear one offers quotes from reviews about five earlier Will James books. But, while the U.S. jacket quotes U.S. reviews, the U.K. jacket quotes different U.K. reviews of the same five books!

Pages: *Flint Spears* starts at Chapter One and page 1, and the numbered text pages end at page 269. Following that are 19 text pages and 18 photograph pages, all unnumbered. There is one free endpaper at the front of the book and one at the back.

Illustrations: Will James illustrated every one of his 24 titles and 27 books with his own drawings and he did so with this book as well. But, in this one book he included 18 pages of 21 photographs of his own choosing to further explain the differences between rodeo and the range. The first of these also appears on the rear panel of the dust wrapper. In addition to the photos, this book has one full-color frontispiece that is also in full color on the dust wrapper, and 30 b&w drawings. Among those 30 are some really fine action drawings that have never appeared in his previous books.

Story #1 — THE FIRST ROUND UP

Pages 1 to 19, with two drawings.
The first cowboy bucking and roping contest is postulated here. And we are introduced to the central character of all the following stories, Flint Spears.

Story #2 — FIRST FIRST PRIZE
    Pages 20 to 41, with two drawings.

Those first bucking and roping contests are concluded to the satisfaction of all.

Story #3 — CONTESTANT SPIRIT
    Pages 42 to 55, with two drawings.
    The herds are loaded onto the rail cars and sent to market. The cowboys disperse to other ranges and winner Flint looks to find a ranch where he can improve on his bronc riding and contesting skills. He hooks up with the '45' outfit and gets introduced to the very tough 'Morte' bunch of broncs. They sure do sharpen him.

Story #4 — THE COWBOY CONTEST FIRST COMES TO TOWN

Pages 56 to 83, with two drawings. A riding contest is put on in a nearby town and Flint comes in second which hurts his pride some. But he teams up with the winner, Mark, and talks him into coming back to the 45 ranch, where he too could benefit from the Morte string and Flint could watch and learn from him.

Story #5 — ALL GATHERED TO WIN
Pages 84 to 95, with two drawings.

The very tough Morte horses are sold en masse to a man named Hurst who envisioned that putting on roping and bucking riding exhibitions could be turned into entertainment that people would pay money to see. When the Morte horses are sold for contest work, Flint and Mark want to go along with them in hopes of winning some of the prize money to be offered. So Hurst hires the two of them to take care of the stock at, and between, contests.

Story #6 — THE MORTE STRING
Pages 96 to 119, with two drawings.
This story is more about bucking horse contests and makes the point that you have to have a really good and tough mount to show up well at the finish. A good rider named Nat joins Flint and Mark and the three of them pretty well dominate the field in bronc riding.

Story #7 — THE COWBOY CONTESTS ARE ON
        Pages 120 to 140, with two drawings.

Lots more contests are put on and additional events added, like steer wrestling and riding, wild horse racing, and so on. Also clowns are included, crooked promoters introduced, and other foofaraw added. Because Flint is dominant in the Bronc riding, Nat and Mark start entering the newer events. Win some of them too.

Story #8 — A RODEO CROSSES THE OCEAN
        Pages 141 to 161, with two drawings.
        The name 'rodeo' is first used. Flint gets a badly crushed and broken leg that lays him up for seven months, but he recovers in time for the European jaunt. That first foreign contest gets aborted in the middle but Flint does well in the first half. He also does well on the return to the States. Girl bronc riding contests are introduced.

Story #9 — MAKING IT TOUGHER ON THE COWBOY
Pages 162 to 175,
with two drawings.
Rodeo rules are
made tougher and
standard saddles
are introduced.

Story #10 — IT'S ALL IN THE GAME
Pages 176 to 200,
with two drawings.

Flint gets a wider reputation
as a top contestant. Friend
Mark is badly hurt and laid
up, so his trick-riding and
Bronc-riding wife, Judy,
comes east to a big show
hoping to win enough con-
test money to help pay the
bills. Flint gives her a hand
when she needs it.

Story #11 — CHAMPION ALL-AROUND COWBOY
Pages 201 to 221, with two drawings.

Flint has won a lot all year,
and at this big eastern
12-day rodeo he wins a lot
more: *Individual Champion
Saddle Bronc Rider* and *All-
Around Cowboy Champion-
ship.* Judy does well too,
till the finals. Then gets
killed in an accident on her
finals ride.

Story #12 — ALL FOR ONE, ONE FOR ALL

Pages 222 to 239, with two drawings. Flint takes Judy's horse, equipment, and remains back to husband Mark at their ranch and stays on for a while to help see Mark through the roughest of his grief.

Story #13 — THE SQUAREST GAME

Pages 240 to 257 with three drawings. The final few years of contesting get harder and harder for Flint, and younger cowboys are coming on very strong. But Flint is still mighty tough and after about his tenth year of major contesting he finishes up at the big 12-day eastern rodeo with top prizes in three events. He gets firsts in steer roping and bronc riding and again is crowned *The World's All-Around Champion Cowboy.*

Story #14 — THE LAST ROUND UP
Pages 258 to 269, with two drawings.

Flint builds the start of his own little ranch in the warmer ranges near the two big outfits he had mostly worked for in the past dozen winters. He also has his eye on a nearby rancher's daughter. At the end of the chapter he decides to retire from major contesting, build up his ranch, and also build up his nerve to ask 'Roberta' to come share the outfit with him.

The final unnumbered pages of the book are devoted to the rodeo rules, photos, and captions.

Later Editions: A Scribner's second printing was issued in 1938, the same as the first except it says "Second Printing, November 1938" under the copyright. It has the 18 pages of rodeo photos. If Scribner's reprinted it after 1938, I haven't seen such.

World Publishing Co. 'Forum Books Edition' produced a reprint saying "First printing March 1946"; brown cloth covers; 8-3/8" by 5-7/8", 269 pages. In October 1948 'World Reprint Edition' put out an edition with gray covers; 8-1/4" x 5-5/8", 269 pages.

Both of these World reprints were produced without the 18 pages of rodeo photos at the back end of the book.

THE DARK HORSE
1939

Contents: This is Will James' final novel and it is a nice one. The central theme horses win in their respective fields, and the rancher's daughter actually marries the cowboy and before the end of the story too! Although the book is certainly a novel, each chapter has a title, and most could stand alone as separate short stories with little or no change.

Comments: Although the leading character is a race horse, only two of the 15 chapters actually involve racing. At least six or seven of the

middle chapters are almost entirely about mustangs and mustanging. Those subjects have always been among Will's favorites; mine too!

First Edition: The first edition of *Dark Horse* was issued in a single state with 1939 at the bottom of the title page and the Scribner's 'A' under the copyright.

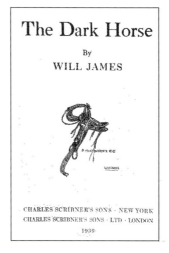

Size & Price: 8-1/2" high, by 6" deep, by 1-1/2" thick. Price: $2.50

Binding: Scribner's bound this in a strong green cloth and all the printing on the binding is in black ink. The front cover has the title at the top and author at the bottom. The spine has title and author at the top and Scribners at the bottom.

Dust Jacket: The dj is in full color and is the same picture as the full color frontispiece in the book. There are two horses standing in a fenced grassy pasture with a desert butte in the left background; the grass and butte wrap around onto the spine. Title and author are at the top of the front cover and Will James' small signature is in the bottom right-hand corner of the picture. The spine has title and author at the top but the Scribners name is just above the middle of the spine in order not to appear in the wrap-around full-color illustration. This is most unusual but a nice touch. The rear cover of the dj has the big-hatted portrait of Will's face that first appeared on the back of *The Three Mustangeers'* dj and was then repeated on many of the subsequent

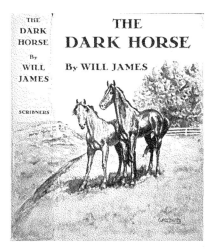

books' djs. The back panel also lists and promotes eight of the previous Will James titles. The front foldover promotes *The Dark Horse,* and the rear one, *Flint Spears.*

Pages: Starting at Chapter One, page 1, the book ends at page 306. There is a single free front endpaper and one at the rear.

Illustrations: *The Dark Horse* has one full-color frontispiece, which is the same illustration as that on the dust jacket, and 38 b&w drawings. The drawing on the title page is a small copy of the one on page 109. All the drawings are original for this book.

Later Editions: Scribner's made a second printing in 1939 <u>without</u> the 'A'. Same size, format, and covers as the first. That's the only Scribner's reprint I've seen.

Grosset & Dunlap reprinted it several times — one with the code 39 and two issues with code 49, but different dust jackets.

The code 39 copy: tan cloth, 8-1/4 x 5-3/4,
277 pages.

First code 49 copy: tan cloth, 8-1/4 x 5-3/4,
277 pages.

Second code 49 copy: gray cloth, same
dimensions and pages.

MY FIRST HORSE
1940

Contents: This is a straight children's picture book and
story. Here Will James amplifies the myth of
his earliest years, first introduced ten years
before.

Comments: My First Horse first edition in dj is just about
the most rare and dear Will James book, even
though also one of the least significant of the
24 titles. In all my years I've only had three of
them in djs and only know of three others in
the hands of collectors. Children's book djs
seldom survive if they were actually ever in
the hands of a child recipient. Even without
the dj this title is
rare and dear, first
or later printing.

First Edition: The
first edition of *My
First Horse* was
produced in a
single state with
1940 at the bottom
of the title page
and the Scribner's
'A' on the overleaf.

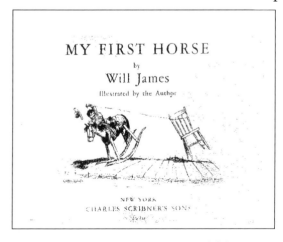

Size & Price: 7-1/4" high, by 9-3/4" deep, by 1/2" thick. Price: $2.00

Binding: The book is bound in blue cloth with title and author near the top of the front cover, and a line drawing of the third color plate in the book near the bottom left of the cover. The writing and sketch are in black ink and there is no writing on the spine of this book.

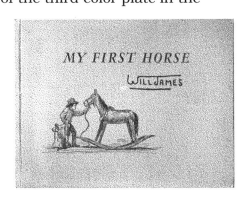

Dust Jacket: The dj is white paper stock that is salmon-colored on three-quarters of the front panel and on all of the spine and rear panel. The sketch from the fifth colored plate in the book is on the front of the dj, and title and author in black ink are at the top on the salmon background. There is no printing on spine and back. The front foldover describes the book while the rear one promotes *Young Cowboy* and *Cowboy in the Making.*

135

Pages: The pages of this book are not numbered. Following the third title page there are 20 full-page tinted plates, and opposite each plate is the text of the story. There are 20 plate pages and 20 text pages in all. There is one free endpaper at the front of the book and there are two at the rear.

Illustrations: To repeat as stated above, the front cover of this book has a line sketch in black ink from the picture in tinted plate three of the book. The title page has a reduced reproduction of tinted plate five, and there are 20 full-page tinted plates in the book.

Later Editions: Scribner's made two second printings of the book in 1940, so it must have had a good reception in its first and only year. Both second printings are the same as the first edition between the covers, with 1940 at the base of the title page but <u>without</u> the Scribner's 'A'. Also the bindings are different. Both have the same printing and picture on the front cover but are bound in green cloth: one in pale green cloth with no printing on the back cover, the other in deeper green cloth with a small horse's head 'Boots & Saddles' logo in the center of the back cover. No other reprints were ever produced, although a few faked copies in very dark green bindings were distributed some years ago.

Horses I've Known
1940

Contents: There are 14 excellent new short stories here, none ever previously included in Will James' earlier books.

Comments: Although nearly the last of Will's books, this one is among the best of his short story works. It hits dead center on his lifelong love of and for all kinds of horses.

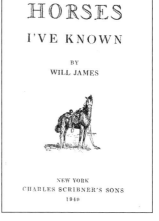

First Edition: The first edition of this title is the only Scribner's edition. And that's mighty strange because it is surely one of Will James' very best short story books. It has 1940 at the bottom of the title page and has the 'A' under the copyright.

Size & Price: 8-1/2" high, by 6" deep, by 1-3/8" thick. Price $2.50

Binding: Bound in gray cloth with the printing on cover and spine in red ink. Title is at the top and author at the bottom of the front cover. Title and author are at the top of the spine and Scribners is at the bottom.

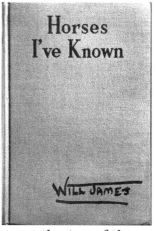

Dust Jacket: The name of this book is *Horses I've Known*. Obviously whoever designed the dust jacket didn't bother with that and renamed it *'Horses I Have Known'*! They repeated that error in all three places where it appears on the dj. The white paper dj has a yellow spine and the yellow also is under the title at the top of the front cover. The full-color frontis-piece in the book is reproduced on the front cover of the dj with the title and author just above the 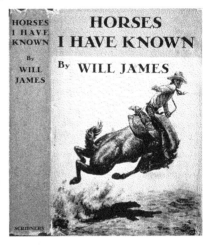 picture. The title and author are at the top of the spine too, with Scribners at the bottom as usual. The rear panel of the dj has the big-hatted portrait of Will's face and advertises eight previous WJ titles. The front foldover has a very fine description of the book, while the rear one promotes *The Dark Horse*. All the printing on the dj is in black ink.

Pages: The first story starts at page 1 and the final story ends with an unnumbered full-page drawing following page 280. The front of the book has two free endpapers and the rear has two also.

Illustrations: There are 33 separate b&w drawings and one full-color frontispiece in the book. As Scribner's states in its description, "Will James illustrates this text with better draw-ings than he has done for a long time."

Story #1 — THE SEEING EYE
   Pages 1 - 25, with two drawings.

This is one of the finest of all Will James' stories. It has been separated out and included in several 'Great Horse Story' anthologies, and in some general subject 'Great Short Story' groupings as well. It is too good a tale to describe, just you read it and 'see' for yourself.

Story #2 — JONES' BEARCAT
   Pages 26 - 43, with two drawings.
   A straight bucking-horse story, and a good one. This story will particularly appeal to anyone who has ridden a whole lot and run into some 'thinking' broncs.

Story #3 — BORROWED HORSES

Pages 44 - 69, with two drawings. Cowboy hi-jinks, in town and out to a country dance with two gals and a 'borrowed' team of horses. The team furnished them with a couple of runaways and that sure broke the ice with the girls. All ends well in spite of a few hours in jail!

Story #4 — FOR THE SAKE OF FREEDOM
Pages 70 - 90, with two drawings.

Mostly a mustang story with detail on the fact that a lot of high desert country, too rocky and too far from water for cows, is still good range for wild horses. (It still is both today.) The story also describes the 'homing instinct' in some horses, and the difficulties and hundreds of miles they'll go through to get back to their home range.

Story #5 — CHAPO - THE FAKER
Pages 91 - 107, with two drawings. About a bronc circle horse who had a full bag of tricks against the rider.

Story #6 — THE TWO GHOSTS
Pages 108 - 128, with two drawings.

It is hoped that modern generations will realize that when this was written 'nigger' was part of the language and used without disrespect more often than not. Most all cowboys loved a joke and some were rough jokes too. This tale is about a joke by two cowboys aimed at the two colored boys newly in camp. The joke started out well enough but then backfired onto the two perpetrators.

Story #7 — MONTE AND THE JACK
Pages 129 - 166, with three drawings.
A good rambling tale about how a cowboy got left afoot out in the middle of nowhere when a big Jack (jackass)

attacked and drove off his hobbled horse. It goes on to tell some of the difficulties the cowboy went through to first get back to civilization, and then get back his horse.

Story #8 — CLUBFOOT
Pages 167 - 187, with two drawings.
A bucking horse and green rider story with a happy ending for both.

141

Story #9 — ONE GOOD TURN
Pages 188 - 202,
with two drawings.
Croppy was a
good little horse
that turned into
a camp follower,
and he sure
bailed his cowboy
out of a tight
spot in this yarn.

Story #10 — "BOARHOUND" (A circle horse)

Pages 205 - 221, with two
drawings.
Light and easy, short
and sweet. A bucking-
horse story with its own
special variety of differences.

Story #11 — HIPPY (A night
horse)
Pages 222 - 237,
with two drawings.
This pony has
brains, and
imagination too.
There is also a
roundup cook
who is not
happy.

Story #12 — THE BUCKING HORSE
Pages 238 - 250, with one drawing.

For a wonder, that one drawing isn't of a bucking horse! This is less a story than a statement of Will's oft-held philosophy about bucking horses, about what makes them and what doesn't. He does finish off with a description of how one particular bronc got into the rodeo game, and excelled there.

Story #13 — JOKER (A horse that lived up to his name)
Pages 251 - 268, with two exceptionally graphic and very good drawings. Another nice little horse's tale as only Will can dream them up.

143

Story #14 — HORSES I'LL NEVER FORGET
Pages 269 - 280, with three drawings.

Here Will finishes this book with a thumbnail sketch of his actual three favorite horses: Smoky, Big Enough, and Comet. Any cowboy who has had even one or two great horses in his lifetime is pretty lucky; Will James had three and that's 'going some.'

Later Editions: There are no known Scribner's reprints of this book. World Publishing reprinted it at least three times, all 8-3/8" by 6", 281 pages, red cloth covers. All three are only half as thick as the Scribner's books. Amusingly, World copied exactly the same title confusion that Scribner's started — printing 'Horses I've Known' throughout the book and 'Horses I _Have_ Known' in three places on their dust jacket!

FORUM BOOKS Edition, first printing, May 1945

FORUM BOOKS Edition, second printing, November 1945

THE WORLD PUBLISHING COMPANY Edition, first printing, May 1948

No other publisher has reprinted this book up to this writing.

THE AMERICAN COWBOY
1942

Contents: This rambling narrative is a series of connecting short stories about three cowboys, first named Billy and then Bill. The narrative ends with Will's article of faith: "The Cowboy Will Never Die."

Comments: The best way to describe the book appears in Will James' preface to it. To quote one paragraph:

> "There's no datas [sic] or such like to bother with in this story. The important thing to me is to take this cowboy through in three generations, with what he had to put up with to hold his cattle and range, from the 1830's up to the present generation, to the cowboy of today."

Quite a lot of the material in this string of stories has been reworked from previous things Will had written, particularly in *Lone Cowboy* and *Smoky.* But the book holds together well and, in my view, it does what his preface promised.

First Edition: This is Will James' final book as he wrote them. There is only one state of the first edition and it has the 1942 date at the bottom of the title page and the 'A' under the copyright.

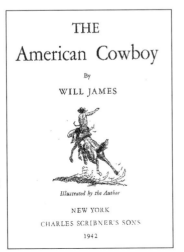

THE

American Cowboy

By

WILL JAMES

Illustrated by the Author

NEW YORK

CHARLES SCRIBNER'S SONS

1942

Size & Price: 8-1/2" high, by 6" deep, by 1-1/2" thick. Price: $2.50

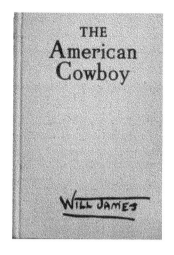

Binding: The book is attractively bound in brilliant red cloth with the writing on cover and spine in midnight blue ink. The cover has the title at the top and author at the bottom, and the spine has title and author at the top and Scribners at the bottom.

Dust Jacket: The dj is light tan paper with a very fine full color picture on most of the front cover, leaving room only at the top for title and author. The picture shows a cowboy driving a little bunch of cattle. The spine and back panel are printed with a yellow sand background and the spine has three horizontal red bands, one at the top, one at the bottom, and one under the author. Title and author are between the

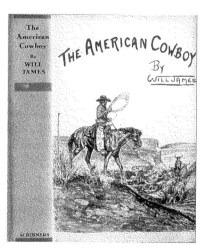

two top red bands and Scribners is tight over the bottom one. The rear panel of the dj has the often-used portrait of Will in his big cowboy hat and advertises eight of the earlier Will James books. Black ink is used for the portrait and all the writing, front, back and spine. The front foldover is Scribner's pitch for the book and the rear one touts *Horses I've Known.*

146

Pages: Chapter One starts at page 1 and the book ends on page 273. There is one free endpaper at the front and one at the back of the book.

Illustrations: All 50 of the illustrations in this book are b&w line drawings. A number of the drawings were in earlier books of his, but a number of good ones appear here for the first time. He could still put out good stuff in this last year of his life. It is interesting to me, and most unusual, that this book has no frontispiece, and also not one colored illustration in the book. It would have enhanced the book a whole lot to at least have put in the very nice dj cover painting as a frontispiece, as Scribner's had done to brighten up several others of Will's books. The dj only infrequently survives the book in most Will James' titles, although with this particular book it survives more often than one would expect.

Story #1 — "THE FIRST COWBOY"

Pages 1 - 13, with three drawings.

This first story starts with Billy, orphaned by an Indian massacre in the Texas territory at about age 10, heading out afoot and on his own. He gets semi-adopted by a professional buffalo hunter and then works his way up to becoming the first cowboy to aim a herd of cattle for the new railroad in Abilene.

Story #2 — "TRAILS FORK"

Pages 14 - 42, with four drawings.

Billy gathers some restless settler boys of about his own age of 20 or so, and they manage to put together a little herd of wild longhorn cattle and head north. Through floods, Indians, and a couple of lesser disasters they manage to make it to the rail head with about half of the crew and half of the cattle surviving; the first herd to make it up from Texas. Bill pioneered other routes and treks with  larger herds, first to Abilene, then to Dodge City and beyond. He included drives to the Colorado mining towns and then even went up as far as the Canadian border. Bill set up his own ranch in the tall grass Montana territory and some of his trail crony cowboys took places in the vicinity. This episode ends with Bill heading west toward the coast on a horse-buying trip, getting a good bunch along with a nice girl, Donna. He brings Donna back to the ranch as his wife and brings along the good string of horses too.

Story #3 — "AN ARROW"

Pages 43 - 65, with five drawings.

Things go pretty well for a while on the new northern ranches. But then the Indians get

stirred up by the soldiers and take it out on the ranchers. Indian war parties tackle Bill's ranch a few times but he always manages to beat them off, although they put an arrow in Donna's shoulder in one of the raids. When the Indian troubles settle down, then come the sheep men - that starts another battle.

Story #4 — "THE SCOURGE"
Pages 66 - 85, with four drawings.
After the sheep came the sodbusters (The Homestead Act), then rustlers, and also the cattle wars over range rights. Being a cowman always was and still is a rough game, but Bill persevered and Donna gave him a son, Billy.

Story #5 —"ON THE MIDDLE RIDGE"

Pages 86 - 109, with three drawings.

The cow coun-
try grows up
some and so
does young
Billy. He
takes more to
range work
than to school
work but
Donna sees to
it that he gets
some school-
ing too. A very
tough winter
converts Bill
to cutting

some wild hay which he had not done much
of before. But he has started breeding up his
herd with imported Hereford bulls and the
new breed isn't as tough as his old beloved
longhorns — does better at market though.

Story #6 —"THE COWBOY RIDES ON"

Pages 110 - 120, with three drawings.

Times are changing
and Bill and
Donna get
elderly and
then older.
When they
cross 'the
great divide'
young Billy is
full grown and
in charge;
he's BILL now.

Story #7 — "SEGUNDO"

Pages 121 - 141, with five drawings.
Everything runs smoothly on the ranch for a while and Bill gets restless. He hasn't seen much of the country and wants to. So he leaves the place in charge of his 'Segundo' (foreman) and rambles for quite a spell.

Story #8 — "RIDING ON"

Pages 142 - 164, with four drawings.
In his rambles Bill stumbles onto a small ranch run by two ladies, mother and grown daughter, Carol, who need a helping hand. He steps in and helps, even to doing ranch work afoot for the first time. He sure doesn't care for that much but gets it done. He gets them back on their feet and then rides on.

Story #9 — "AS THE SNOW CAME"
    Pages 165 - 184, with three drawings.

Bill picks up a traveling partner and they ride south to get away from the cold northern winter. They end up way south where they get their horses and tack stolen!

Story #10 — "AFOOT BUT NOT WALKING"
    Pages 185 - 211, with four drawings.

The two cowboys come to the conclusion that their host for that night was responsible for the stealing of their outfit. So they 'talk him' into returning it. Bill's partner then suggests a side trip to the movie studios in Hollywood where the pay may be pretty good but Bill doesn't take to the work much. So he's off for a brief jaunt to Mexico. Then a short stretch in Texas, and on back north.

Story #11 — "REGULAR FOLKS"

Pages 212 - 229, with two drawings.

Bill does more rambling on the way back to his home ranch where he finds that everything is in good order. Except there he finds an overdue army service draft notice requiring him to hightail it into the army for World War I.

Story #12 — "ATTENTION"

Pages 230 - 247, with two drawings.

After a few weeks of drilling on foot, he graduates to 'topping off' the officers' mounts, horses that they frequently find too rough for their handling. From there Bill gets 'volunteered' into the Remount Inspection Branch where he gets to constantly ride the rough new outlaw recruit horses.

Story #13 — "DISARMAMENT"

Pages 248 - 257, with two drawings. This one covers Bill's last army days, his 'demobbing', and his return to his ranch.

Story #14 — "THE COWBOY WILL NEVER DIE"
Pages 258 - 273, with three drawings.

With his discharge Bill reminisces for a while, then finally gets his priorities straight and heads back to get Carol. Her mother has died and her foreman is handling things fine, so she and Bill get hitched and head back to his ranch. Billy the 3rd comes along in due course, soon to become a cowboy like his dad and granddad before him. **The Cowboy Will Never Die**" are the last words in the book.

Later Editions: Scribner's republished this book several times in the same general size and format:

Scribner's 1943 - shiny red cover.

Scribner's 1945 - tan cover and wartime thinner.

Scribner's after 1951 - perhaps 1963, red cover.

Scribner's after 1951 - perhaps 1970, red cover.

No other publishers' copies of this book have come before my eyes.

Will James' Book of Cowboy Stories
1951

Contents: Here is a loose group of 15 short stories, all of which had appeared in earlier Scribner's Will James books. They are listed by their 1951 title and earlier book use. Where the title is new, the original title will be included in the description that follows it.

Comments: Scribner's says on the front foldover of the first-edition dj of this book that they selected these stories from all the Will James books, and that the many drawings have also been selected from the best in all the books. Poor Will must have rolled over in his ashes at that desecration. He most frequently made the pictures to illustrate the text. Many of these are far from his best stories, and some have been edited brutally. As for the chosen pictures, most don't follow the storyline at all! It's a wicked shame. This book was put together in 1951, nine years after Will's funeral. I can only think that the good Scribner's editors of the 1920s and '30s must have died too.

First Edition: The first edition has 1951 over the 'Sons' of Scribner's Sons at the bottom of the title page. That, and the 'A' under the copyright, are only found in the one first-edition state. Scribner's did several reprints, as you will see below, but none of them has either of those features.

WILL JAMES'
BOOK OF COWBOY STORIES

NEW YORK   1951
ILLUSTRATED BY WILL JAMES   CHARLES SCRIBNER'S SONS

Size & Price: 8-1/2" high, by 6-7/8" deep, by 7/8" thick. Price: $2.50

Binding: A handsome little book bound in rust-colored cloth with the printing on the spine and the silhouette sketch on the front cover standing out sharply in bright white ink. The only printing is on the spine, just the full title along it and Scribners in smaller type at the end.

Dust Jacket: Pale cream-colored paper mostly covered with soft brown ink and with nearly all the lettering offset on the covers and spine. The cowboy-hatted portrait of Will's face is on the front panel in black ink and the title is under it in white. There is a black ink rope border on the back panel with the Boots and Saddles logo at the bottom. Offset inside the border are six Will James titles and six horse book titles by other

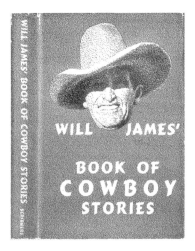

Scribner's authors, including two by Paul Brown. The spine of the dj has only title and Scribners, the same as on the binding. The front foldover extols the virtues of Will's writing and drawings. It says these were taken from all his books, but that's an exaggeration. The rear foldover is a biographical sketch even more mythical than that in his *Lone Cowboy* autobiography!

Pages: Story #1 starts on page 1 and the final story, #15, ends on page 242. There is one free endpaper at the front and one at the back of the book.

Illustrations: The title page in this book is a double-page spread of the very fine two-page drawing that is on pages 2 and 3 of *Flint Spears* and illustrates the first chapter of that book. Besides the silhouette on the front cover and the double title page, there are 30 separate b&w drawings in the book. One of them, the chapter heading drawing, is used 15 times. There is not even one colored illustration included in the book.

Story #1 — ON THE DRIFT

Pages 1 - 10, with three illustrations, none of which were in the original story.

First book appearance was in *All in the Day's Riding*, Chapter 5.

Story #2 — THE BEST RIDING AND ROPING

Pages 11 - 39, with three drawings.

At least they used the proper drawings in this story, which was originally published in *Flint Spears* as Chapter 1 and titled 'The First Round Up,' and Chapter 2, titled 'The First Prize.'

Story #3 — WINTER MONTHS IN A COW CAMP

Pages 40 - 58.

Three of the six original drawings appeared in *Cowboys North and South* under the same title.

Story #4 — LONE COWBOY

Pages 59 - 70 with one picture.

This story was taken from most of Chapter 10 of the book *Lone Cowboy* and the one picture in this story was not in that book.

Story #5 — SMOKY, THE RANGE COLT

Pages 71 - 81, with two drawings.
First published as
Chapter 1 in
Smoky; an
edited
version also
appeared in
*The Will
James
Cowboy
Book* 1938.
This story
in 1951 was
further
edited from
Chapters 1
and 2.  The 1926 and 1938 stories included
several really dandy pictures of the young
Smoky. The two drawings in this 1951 book
don't even pretend to fit the storyline.

Story #6 — THE MAKINGS OF A COWHORSE

Pages 82 - 97, with two drawings from the original
six as first published in *Cowboys North and South.*
This story was also reprinted in *Sun Up.*

Story #7 — CHAPO - THE FAKER
Pages 98 - 109.
First published in
Horses I've Known;
there is one draw-
ing included here
but it is not one of
the original ones.

Story #8 — A NARROW ESCAPE
Pages 110 - 116,
with no pictures!
The first book
publication of this
story was in *All in
the Day's Riding* and it was then titled 'Down
the Wash.' It also was in *The Will James
Cowboy Book* 1938, with the new title as
above. As first produced, it was so graphically
and well illustrated that you could see the
whole story from the pictures. To reproduce it
without at least one of the fine illustrative
pictures seems to me just downright silly.

Story #9 — WHEN IN ROME—
Pages 117 - 137, with one drawing.

As usual in this book, the drawing is not one of those used in the story as first published in *Cow Country*, which had four pictures very much tied in with the text. This piece, properly illustrated, was also included in the *Sun Up* collection of stories.

Story #10 — FOR A HORSE

Pages 138 - 150. One very good drawing is in-

cluded from those originally in the *All in the Day's Riding* version, the first appearance of this tale.

It is a very, very good Will James story but he may have had second thoughts about writing it, because it sure raises questions about one of his pet and often repeated positions that bucking horses are born, not made. It's a mighty fine read; try it.

Story #11 — SILVER MOUNTED

Pages 151 - 171. Two drawings, one of which is from the original version in *Cow Country*. 'Silver Mounted' also appeared in *Sun Up*.

Story #12 — ON THE DODGE

Pages 172 - 194, with two unrelated drawings.
First appearing in book form in *Sun Up,* this
story and
the one that
follows it
here are
better suited
to pulp
magazines
than to a
book of the
supposedly
representa-
tive, and
better, Will
James tales.

Story #13 — CATTLE RUSTLERS

Pages 195 - 208. Three of the seven drawings in
the original *Cowboys North
and South* story are included.
One of the best features of
the original story, about
teaching a nester the
etiquette involved in
butchering someone else's
beef, is entirely omitted in
this desecration! (The
editor here should be
given a little of the nester's
medicine.) The original
and full story was also in
Sun Up.

Story #14 — FOR THE SAKE OF FREEDOM
Pages 209 - 224, with two unlikely drawings.

This story first saw print in magazine form under the title of 'Wild Freedom.' The first book appearance was in *Horses I've Known*. It was titled 'For the Sake of Freedom,' and it had two good, descriptive drawings in that book.

Story #15 — ONCE A COWBOY
Pages 225 - 242, with two nice drawings. Neither drawing was among the five in the original *Drifting Cowboy* version.

Later Editions: Scribner's reprinted this title at least five times, including one paperback edition.

1956 - Same size as first, brown cloth covers - price ?

1960 - Same size and brown cloth covers - price $2.95

1962 - Paperback green-and-orange printed cover - price $1.25 (This is one of the few Will James books ever produced in paperback by Scribner's.)

1963 - Same as first, salmon cloth cover - price $2.75

1964 - Same as first again — (At the bottom of the dj front foldover it states: Reinforced Binding.) price $5.95

No other publisher has produced this book (for good reason I say).

Appendix A

Short Stories of Will James – Listed and Indexed

A few words of explanation on how to use this chapter. The books are listed below in order of publication, and each title is followed by the year it was first published and its type:

TSS stands for Titled Short Stories.

N stands for Novel or Novelette.

This chapter deals only with the 12 Will James book titles that include the Titled Short Story form. Where there are two TSS books in the same year, the first published one is designated (a) and the second one (b). This only occurs in 1938.

Cowboys North & South	1924 - TSS	In the Saddle	1935 - N
The Drifting Cowboy	1925 - TSS	Young Cowboy	1935 - N
Smoky	1926 - N	Home Ranch*	1935 - TSS
Cow Country	1927 - TSS	Scorpion	1936 - N
Sand	1929 - N	Cowboy In The Making	1937- TSS
Smoky, Classic	1929 - N	Look-See with Uncle Bill	1938 - N
Lone Cowboy	1930 - N	Will James' Cowboy Book	1938 - TSS (a)
Sun-Up	1931 - TSS	Flint Spears*	1938 - TSS (b)
Big Enough	1931 - N	The Dark Horse**	1939 - N
Uncle Bill	1932 - N	My First Horse	1940 - N
Lone Cowboy, Classic	1932 - N	Horses I've Known	1940 - TSS
All In the Day's Riding	1933 - TSS	The American Cowboy*	1942 - TSS
The Three Mustangeers	1933 - N	W.J. Bk. of Cowboy Stories	1951 - TSS

* These three books are novels but have titled chapters that easily make stand-alone stories.
** This novel has titled chapters, but the story line is continuous; chapters don't stand alone.

After each story in the following list of 161 Titled Short Stories, the date following the story identifies the TSS book(s) where you will find that story. Where there are two or more dates shown, that story is in two or three separate Will James books; for example:

> ***Makings of a Cow-horse, The,*** is to be found in *Cowboys North and South* (1924), *Sun Up* (1931), and *Will James Book of Cowboy Stories* (1951).

THE WILL JAMES BOOKS

STORY NAME	YEAR	STORY NAME	YEAR
First Round-Up, The	1938 (b)	Last Round-Up, The	1938 (b)
Folks West	1933	Longhorns, The	1924
For a Horse	1933, 1951	Making it Tougher on the Cowboy	1938 (b)
For the Sake of Freedom	1940, 1951	Makings of a Cow-Horse, The	1924, 1931, 1951
From the Ground Up	1933		
Gros and Otay	1937	March–The First Blades of Green	1933, 1938 (a)
Hard Winters and Dry Summers	1935		
Hell and High Water	1935	May– The Spring Round-Up	1933, 1938 (a)
Hippy (A Night Horse)	1940		
His Spurs	1931	Midnight	1931
His Waterloo	1925, 1931	Monte and the Jack	1940
		Monty of the "Y" Bench	1927
Hold Your Horses	1935	Morte String, The	1938 (b)
Home Guard, A	1931	My First Rifle	1937
Home Ranch	1937	Narrow Escape, A	1938 (a), 1951
Hooks	1933		
Horseflesh	1933	November– The End of the Season	1933, 1938 (a)
Horses and Their Ways	1938 (a)		
Horses I'll Never Forget	1940	October– Cutting Out	1933, 1938 (a)
It's All in the Game	1938 (b)		
Jake Adams, Sourdough	1931	Old Slicker, The	1933
January– Bucking the Drifts, and Looking for Snowbound Stock	1933, 1938 (a)	Old Timer Takes Me Along, The	1937
		On Circle	1933
Jerry's Ornery Streak	1933	On the Dodge	1931, 1951
Joker (A Horse that Lived Up to His Name)	1940	On the Drift	1933, 1951
Jones' Bearcat	1940		
July– Riding for a Prize	1933, 1938 (a)	On the Middle Ridge	1942
		On the Ranch With Uncle Bill	1938 (a)
June–The Horse Round-Up	1933, 1938 (a)	Once a Cowboy	1925, 1951
Kip and Scootie Have an Adventure	1938 (a)	Once When the Laugh Was on Me	1933
Last Catch, The	1927, 1931	One Good Turn	1940
		One that Won	1933

THE WILL JAMES BOOKS

STORY NAME	YEAR	STORY NAME	YEAR
One Up and Three to Go	1935	Squarest Game, The	1938 (b)
Paper and Pencil	1937	Stampeder, A	1933
Pet Wolves, The	1938 (a)	Strangers to Camp	1935
Piñon and the Wild Ones	1924	Thirty Years' Gathering	1933
Range Blacksmith, The	1933	Tight Squeeze, A	1938 (a)
Range Table Etiquette	1933	Tom and Jerry	1933,
Regular Folks	1942		1938 (a)
Regular Ranch vs. Dude		Trails Fork	1942
Ranch	1937	Turning Point, The	1933
Remuda, The	1933	Two Ghosts, The	1940
Riding Bog	1935	Two Old Timers	1927
Riding On	1942	Uncle Bill Tells a Story	1938 (a)
Rodeo Crosses the Ocean, A	1938 (b)	Up in the Eagle Territory	1933
Rodeo, The	1933	When in Rome	1927,
Round-Up Wagon, The	1933		1931,
Scattered Three Ways	1933		1951
Scattered Tracks	1933	When the Cows Come Home	1935
Scourge, The	1942	When Wages Are Low	1925
Seeing Eye, The	1940	Why the High Heels?	1933
Segundo	1942	Wild Horse, The	1927
September– Line-Riders	1933,	Winter Camp	1937
	1938 (a)	Winter Months in a Cow	
Silver-Mounted	1927,	Camp	1924,
	1931,		1951
	1951	Wound Up	1933
Smoky the Range Colt	1938 (a),	Young Cowboy, A	1938 (a)
	1951	Young Cowboy, The	1931
Some Cowboy Adventures	1938 (a)		
Spring and Round-Ups	1935		

APPENDIX B
Will James Signature Variations

Between 1919 and his death in 1942, Will James changed the signature he used professionally over a dozen times. His publisher, Scribner's, compounded the issue by printing older signatures in newer books. One example of this practice is most obvious in Will's 1924 signature at the bottom of the preface of his first book, *Cowboys North and South*. That exact same signature, which Will never again used after 1924, is at the bottom of the preface of *Horses I've Known* (1940), and it is used with seven other book prefaces between those years!

Will used two different signatures in 1919, 1924, and 1927, and between 1931 and 1932 he used three very different ones.

When signing his name in owners' copies of his books he most often included the '111' and the date with his signature up through 1927. After that year he rarely used the 111 with his signature, but nearly always included the date right up through 1942. Most often the date was abbreviated as '30 or '37, etc.

Following are several pages showing nearly all of his signatures from 1915 through 1942. Most of the signatures shown come from inscribed and/or signed copies of his books that are in my personal collection, a few are from signatures on his drawings.

The variety in Will's professional signatures over the twenty-several years shown is fascinating to me. It is also mighty useful in recognizing the occasional forged signature in a signed book. If the forger has used a signature as printed twice in *Lone Cowboy* for instance, which

169

one did he copy? *Lone Cowboy* has the 1924 signature with the 111 under the frontispiece photo portrait and the 1930 signature under the preface. Neither of them has the date.

Keep in mind that just about always when Will James signed or inscribed one of his books he included the year date when he signed it.

Three closing notes on the subject. Will often signed himself as Bill or Bill James to his wife and close friends. All his professional signatures are in print form. He always signed his personal bank checks with a totally different, cursive, signature.

170

To, Ralph Henry —
Here's two ponies that never
lost their heads —
You take one and I'll take
the other — But we've got
to ride, by Jaysus, H. —" —
  Yours Sincerely
  WILL JAMES
  '39

To, Alice —
With my best wishes
for a happy, healthy and
wealthy New Year.
  Bill

To Dorothy Rayton

Sincerely from.

WILL JAMES
'29

Here's a good loop—

Don't never "spill" it.

1915
IN
Jail

W.R.JAMES ,19

WILL JAMES
III - 19

WILL JAMES
III ~.20

WILLJAMES
III ~ .21

WILLJAMES
III ~.22

WILLJAMES
III ~ 23

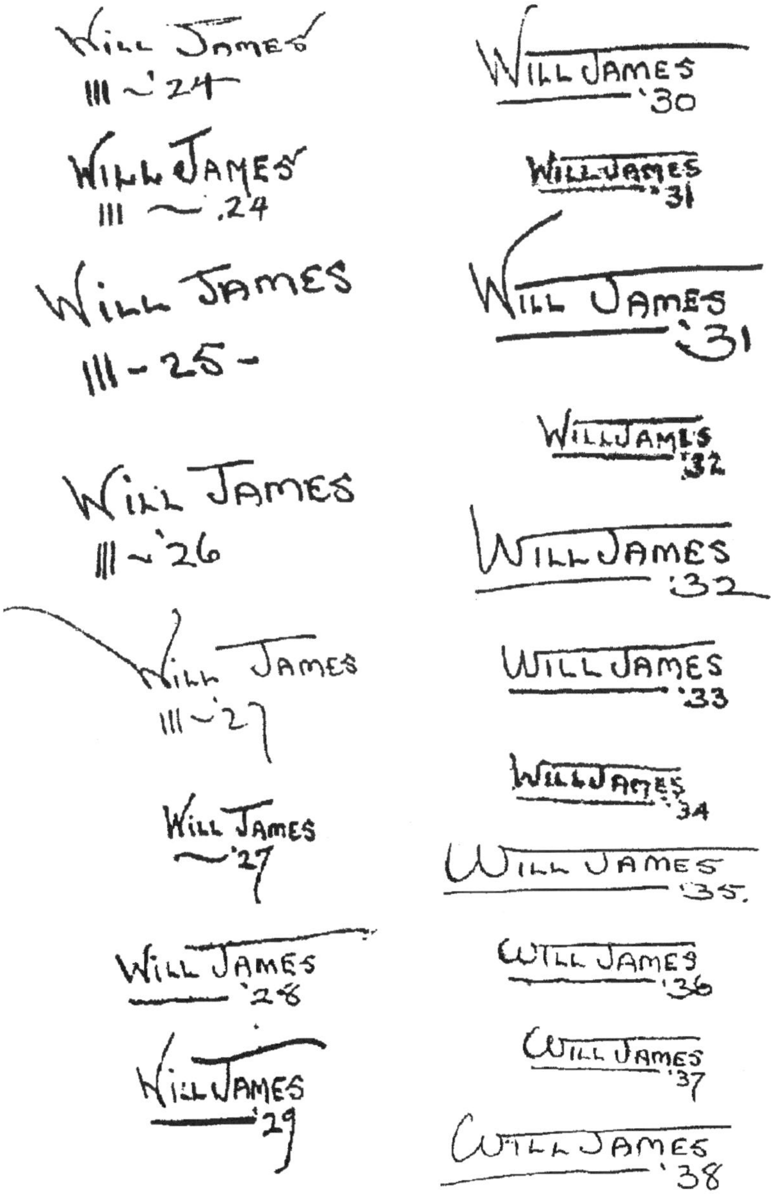

Will James
III ~ '24

Will James
III ~ .24

Will James
III - 25 -

Will James
III ~ '26

Will James
III ~ '27

Will James
~ '27

Will James
'28

Will James
'29

Will James
'30

Will James
'31

Will James
'31

Will James
'32

Will James
'32

Will James
'33

Will James
'34

Will James
'35.

Will James
'36

Will James
'37

Will James
'38

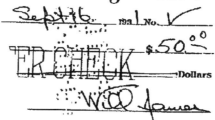

APPENDIX C
Glossary

b&w — black and white (abbreviation).

copyright page — Contains copyright information and is to be found on the back side of the title page. Sometimes it has other as well.

corral — An enclosure for stock. Usually a small pen for close work with horses or cattle.

cow savvy — Very knowing about all the details of working with cattle.

dj or djs — Book dust jacket, dust cover or dust wrapper.

endpaper — The inside of the front and rear covers of a hardbound book have a pasted down sheet that continues on to make the first endpaper. This sheet is usually unprinted; it and additional unprinted sheets are called free endpapers.

ex-lib — Means a 'used library copy' of a book and usually contains clear evidence thereof. It is a serious blemish in the used book trade.

foldovers — The two wrap around ends of a book dust jacket.

foofaraw — Catch-all name for frothy or incidental miscellany.

front footing — To catch a four footed animal by both front feet.

greenhorn — In range parlance any individual new to the range.

ground hitched — Bridle reins over the head and dropped to the ground. Properly trained, a horse will stay put as if tied.

grub line riding — Nomadic traveling from one part of the range to another and stopping at ranches along the way occasionally to exchange news and catch a meal.

175

hackamore	A form of bridle with a headstall and reins plus a noseband in place of a bit in the horse's mouth.
lass rope	Also called a lasso. A long rope of hide (riata), or other material, with a running noose at one end – used for catching horses and cattle, etc.
mustang	The American wild horse
nester	Homesteader, sod-buster, etc.
pagination	How book pages are numbered and described.
paste-downs	The sheets pasted to the inside of the front and rear book covers. The sheet continues to become the first endpaper.
possibles	All, or most all, of a roving cowboy's belongings.
remuda	A holding bunch for the strings of saddle horses that are in use out on the range, as for instance, with a roundup crew.
riata	See 'lass rope' above.
segundo	Ranch foreman, overseer.
sodbusters	Another word for homesteader.
tenderfoot	Another name for greenhorn, a rank novice.
top hand	One of the very best of a group of working cowboys.
top horse	One of the very best of a large remuda of cowhorses.
topping off	In range use it means for an experienced rider to get on a fresh horse and give him a warm-up ride before a less experienced rider gets on.

Afterword – About the Author

Several people have asked what my credentials are for writing a book about Will James books. Of course the answer is that I have almost none, although I did write a quite well-received book on *Recognizing Derrydale Press Books* back in 1983. In place of proper bonafides I simply have a lifelong love of Will James books and the subjects that he loved, drew, and wrote about.

Raised on a large working horse ranch in northern Nevada from age six until I went into the Army Air Corps at age 19 in 1943, I lived at least part of the kind of life that Will did. Our outfit raised horses mostly, usually about 500 head at any one time and we had most kinds — stock horses, work horses, mules, and later, a little bunch of fine Thoroughbreds for hunter/jumpers and race horses. In addition, and more for fun than for profit, we used to run wild horses. There were hundreds of them too close for comfort just north of our line. (A scrub mustang stud getting in with our mares was a disaster.)

My first time running mustangs, they ran me. It was my first year at the ranch, I was about six years old and green as grass. My horse Micky was pretty elderly but had been a fine cow-horse in his day and he still had considerable enthusiasm around

Don on old Micky about 1931

stock. On that first mustang run Micky and I were placed "out of the way" at a good lookout spot and told to "turn the bunch downhill if they come your way." The grown-ups were sure that the wild ones would never come near my perch. But mustangs don't set out to cooperate and they did come tearing through the landscape right by me. In trying to turn them Micky and I got right in the middle of the bunch careening along a rocky draw. We didn't get any mustangs that day but it sure triggered my love for running them.

Our ranch headquarters was 50 narrow, washboardy, and very dusty miles north of Reno and the nearest school, so I had 'home courses' - sometimes! Did end up spending two years at an eastern boarding school, and later earned a high school certificate, but the only college I ever had was the 'hard knocks' variety.

My first Will James book, *Big Enough*, was given to me the year it was written, 1931, on either my seventh birthday or at Christmas, I forget which. It is still my favorite of all. Of course I got and read all seven of the earlier books and thereafter Will's newest publication was always at the top of my birthday and Christmas wish list.

Will James wrote about cowboying as it was a century ago, but also about how it still is in the high desert country of the Great Basin even today. Even a kid could be a fairly useful hand a-horseback some of the time, and as a youngster I did most everything with horses that Will describes. No great shakes as a bronc rider, but rode my share when I couldn't talk them out of misbehaving. I worked and rode in most kinds of horse activities, with stock horses, draft horses, polo ponies, hunters and jumpers, steeplechase and race horses, good ones and bad ones. Fell off, thrown off, stepped out from under and onto in every way known at the time - even invented a few ways no one on the outfit had ever seen before. Broken bones, abrasions, and torn this and that not withstanding, still I could 'get the job done' some way — a credo preached by Will and one I've tried to live by all of my life.

Although I sure enjoyed that life, I went back East after my hitch in the Army Air Corps (1943-46) was over, hoping to learn to be a business man. I had no money or formal training, and all that I knew about horse-ranching had taught me that it was no way to raise a family and make a living in the Depression years that I knew well. Fortunately, though it took a few decades, I did have some success in the business world.

In order to get back to the northern Great Basin country I loved, I then rejuvenated a hobby of my youth and started going out for a few days, then weeks, every year with University of Nevada (Reno) Archaeology crews who were studying the tracks and trails of Early Man in the northern Great Basin. A couple of decades of traipsing about in the northern Nevada and southern Oregon high deserts have allowed me to see for myself that working stock is still done with the horses and skills that Will wrote about and drew so very well 75 years ago. Of course trucks and trailers have speeded up communications some, but the feed for the stock is mostly up in steep rocky country and even the most sophisticated all-terrain vehicles have no hope of doing away with horse and cowboy as long as stock is ranged there.

Even today there are over 30,000 wild horses in Nevada alone, managed by the Federal Bureau of Land Management (BLM), and I've seen hundreds of them every year. They are every bit as wild and beautiful as they ever were. You can't legally run them as we used to but you can adopt good young wild horses that the BLM makes available every year. And there are always some that turn out to be top horses, too.

Still no really good credentials for me, but I am a book lover, and got my early education almost entirely from reading books and working with horses. Also I had ample opportunity to see earlier cowboying in the 1930s, and cowboying today in the 1990s. Many things have changed, but going 'wide open' down a steep and rocky mountainside to head off a bunch of streaking critters still takes a crazy cowboy on a good horse — <u>to get the job done</u>.

Don Frazier
Long Valley, NJ
March 1998